ROBERT PUGH

BLACKLO'S CABAL

1680

With an introduction by
T. A. BIRRELL

1970
GREGG INTERNATIONAL PUBLISHERS LIMITED ENGLAND

S.B.N. − 0.576.78534.2

Republished in 1970 by Gregg International Publishers Limited
Westmead, Farnborough, Hants., England

Printed in offset by Anton Hain KG, Meisenheim/Glan
Western Germany

INTRODUCTION

The first thing to be noted about this volume is the circumstances surrounding its publication in 1680. At the height of the Popish Plot, in 1679, two priests of the English Catholic secular clergy Chapter, John Sergeant and David Maurice, came forward in public as informers against the Jesuits, and it was evident that a small group of English secular priests hoped to obtain toleration from the government by taking the forbidden Oath of Allegiance and by agreeing to the expulsion of the Jesuits. Father John Warner SJ, the Jesuit Provincial at the time, wrote to Cardinal Howard at Rome to urge the Roman authorities to make some explicit declaration against Sergeant and his friends, for "not a Jesuit passes into England, that Mr Sergeant can hear of, but his name is carried to the [Privy] Council, and ... he hath his brethren at or about the sea ports, who give him informations of such things." It was as a measure of retaliation against this state of affairs that Warner published *Blacklo's Cabal*.[1] His aim was to show the consistency of the policy of a small clique within the secular clergy Chapter, Thomas White (or Blacklo), Henry Holden and John Sergeant, whose aim was to bargain with the government of the day, be it Cavalier or Roundhead, to obtain toleration at the price of the exclusion of the Jesuits from England.[2]

The dossier of letters that Warner published had been collected by Robert Pugh (1610–1679), who had been arrested during the Plot and died in Newgate gaol. The dossier had been deposited at the Jesuit College at Ghent and presumably on Pugh's death Warner felt entitled to use it.

---

1. See John Warner's 'History of the Popish Plot', *Catholic Record Society,* vols. 47/48 (1953/55) and M. V. Hay, *The Jesuits and the Popish Plot,* London 1933.

2. The most recent study of Blacklo is R. I. Bradley's unpublished Ph. D. thesis, Columbia 1963; cf. his essay in *From Renaissance to Counter Reformation,* ed. C. H. Carter, London 1966. A chronological account of Blacklo's life by D. Shanahan is appearing in the *Essex Recusant.* It is interesting to note that Sir Kenelm Digby settled an annuity of £ 300 p. a. on Blacklo, which passed to John Sergeant on Blacklo's death (Barrett Papers, Berkshire Record Office). For Henry Holden, see Ruth Clark, *Strangers and Sojourners at Port Royal,* Cambridge 1932. For Sergeant see M. V. Hay, *op. cit.*

Pugh had entered the Society of Jesus, but had been dismissed in 1645 for taking up arms in the Civil War. Though a secular clergyman, he had always been opposed to the anti-Jesuit faction in the Chapter, and had always maintained that the regular clergy should be exempt from the jurisdiction of the Chapter. Pugh had been friendly with Abbot Walter Montagu (1603—1677), chaplain to Queen Henrietta Maria in her exile, and it was through Montagu that Pugh obtained the dossier.[3]

The first group of letters, from 1645 to 1653, centre round Sir Kenelm Digby and his embassy at Rome on behalf of Henrietta Maria.[4] The principal object of Digby's mission to Rome was to secure Papal aid for the English Royalists. The Papal Nuncio Rinuccini had been despatched to the Irish Confederates in 1645. Digby's primary task was to ensure that not all Papal aid went to Ireland, but that something at least went direct to England. Then, after the King's decisive defeat at Naseby in June 1645, all efforts were directed to encouraging a compromise between the Confederacy and the Royalist army in Ireland under the Viceroy Ormond. The difficulty of the whole situation was that, while the Papacy demanded evidence of toleration of Catholicism, the King could not publicly make concessions to the Catholics without antagonizing his Protestant supporters. Furthermore, after Naseby the King was in no position to effectuate any promises he might make, even if he had wished to.[5]

3. An important letter by Pugh under the alias Petrus Hoburgus, an anagram for "Robertus Pughus") to Cardinal Francesco Barberini, dated 13 November 1661, gives a complete survey of the troubles of the English Clergy from 1633 onwards. It is printed in Charles Plowden's *Remarks on a Book Entitled Memoirs of Gregorio Panzani*, Liège 1794, pp. 360—379. A description of Pugh in Welsh is to be found in *Mawl Penrhyn* by William Pugh OSB, (National Library of Wales MS 4710 B f 335) which states,*inter alia*, that Pugh had been tutor to Henry Duke of Gloucester. (I owe this reference to Mr. Geraint Bowen).

4. Two recent works purport to deal with this episode in Digby's career: V. Gabrieli, *Sir Kenelm Digby*, Rome 1957 and R. T. Petersson, *Sir Kenelm Digby*, London 1956. Neither seem to have much understanding of the historical background, and the inaccuracy of Petersson is really irresponsible. That a philosophical *flaneur* like Digby was totally unsuited for any diplomatic mission whatsoever is well borne out by these letters.

5. The primary source for Rinuccini's mission is of course the *Commentarius Rinuccinianus* now published by the Irish Historical Manuscript Commission in 6 vols., Dublin 1932—1949. M. J. Hynes, *The Mission of Rinuccini*, Dublin 1932, is a useful guide.

The principal concerns of Digby's mission hardly emerge in *Blacklo's Cabal*. Instead we find some of Digby's friends in the English secular clergy Chapter using Digby's presence in Rome to try to obtain Papal recognition of the authority of the Chapter, and if possible a bishop (or bishops) for England. Then, when the royal cause is clearly lost, they veer round to try to do a deal with the Cromwellian government.[6] Holden's letters to Digby in 1649, in which he attacks George Leyburne, the Vicar General of Richard Smith, Bishop of Calcedon, and hopes that Leyburne will be arrested by the authorities, are most damning. So too are Digby's dealings with Thomas Watson, scoutmaster to the Army, and his sycophantic pleas to the Government in 1650−1652. In fact the Civil Wars and Commonwealth split the secular clergy Chapter very bitterly. The continental exiles on the whole remained Royalist in sympathy, but there was a definite breakaway movement in England within the Chapter itself, whose supporters wished to disown the authority of the exiled Vicar Apostolic, Bishop Richard Smith. After the Restoration this led to friction between the London Chapter and the President of Douay, Dr. George Leyburne, a staunch Royalist and supporter of Bishop Smith.

The final group of letters in *Blacklo's Cabal* dates from 1667. At this period there were further efforts to obtain a Catholic bishop for England. The Chapter feared that George Leyburne might be appointed and did everything to make his position at Douay untenable. It would seem that the Chapter were hoping for Abbot Walter Montagu as a compromise figure, but he wisely refused to be considered. On the other hand, Montagu had insisted that the Chapter Agent at Rome should present to the Holy See a protestation of loyalty and a disavowal of the theological unorthodoxy of Blacklo. This suggestion was frustrated by John Sergeant, the then Secretary of the Chapter and a staunch supporter

The unpublished London University Ph. D. thesis 1960 by J. Lowe, "Negotiations between Charles I and the Confederation of Kilkenny 1642−49", deals with Henrietta Maria, Urban VIII and Innocent X on pp. 367−408. George Leyburne's *Memoirs*, London 1722, are especially relevant.

6. An important article, by Thomas H. Clancy SJ, on the attitude of the English Catholics towards the Independents in the summer of 1647 is shortly to be published in *Recusant History*. In all fairness to the Chaptermen it must be said that they were not alone in wishing to obtain toleration from the Independents at that juncture. Of course, after 30 January 1649, dealings with the Cromwellian government must be looked on in a different light.

of Blacklo. The trouble over this matter eventually forced Sergeant's resignation as secretary.[7]

Lord Acton included Holden, Blacklo and Sergeant among the handful of "original thinkers among the English Catholics."[8] But the evidence of *Blacklo's Cabal* may serve to put them in a somewhat different perspective.

T. A. BIRRELL

7. See T. A. Birrell, "English Catholics without a Bishop 1655–1672," *Recusant History*, Vol. IV, no. 4 (January 1958), pp. 142–178.

8. *Letters of Lord Acton to Mary Gladstone,* London 1904, p. 140.

BLACKLO'S CABAL

Difcovered in feverall of their

LETTERS

Clearly expreffing DESIGNS
INHVMANE againft Regulars,
VNIVST againft the LAITY,
SCISMATICAL aganift the POPE,
CRVEL againft Orthodox Clergy men
And ovvning
the NVLLITY of the Chapter,
their oppofition of Epifcopall Authority

Publifhed

By R. *PVGH I. V. DOCTOR·*

Nihil abfconditum quod non reuelabitur

The fecond edition enlarged
in fome fevv Notes.

PERMISSV SVPERIORVM.

M D C L X X X.

Republished in 1970 by Gregg International Publishers Limited
Westmead, Farnborough, Hants., England

Printed in offset by Anton Hain KG, Meisenheim/Glan
Western Germany

The Epistle to the Catholick Reader.

I Here present you with a collection of some Letters written by severall of the Prime secular men of our nation : which discouer theirsecret Designs against Regulars, and the Papal Authority in *England*, without sparing those of their own Body , who were not susceptible of their schismaticall spirit as may be seen in their procedure against *Dr. George Leybourn* legally installed their *Vicar General* by the Bishop of Calcedon, whom they endeauord to get killed or at least banisht by the Rebellious Parliament *not for Religion*, but *as a spy, a Broullion, a factious man, and* what else they pleased to represent him to the state.

The Authours of these Letters are Very well known to most of our Ancient clergy men, yet because they may fall into some hands who may be strangers to them I will here giue a short Character of them.

The first; and as it were Primum mobile of all, is Mr *Tomas White* of *Essex*, commonly known by the name of *Blacklo:* who haueing studyed his Humanity at *S Omers*, his Phylosophy, and part of his Diuinity at *Valladolid*, and the rest at *Louen*, all vnder the *Iesuits*, was thence inuited to *Doway* Colledg by Dr Kellison when he set vp schools, to teach Phylosophy, where he began to employ the Doctrine he had learnt Vnder the *Iesuits* to impugn them : yet he profest there only rigid *Thomistry* which name to auoyd that of a nouellist he affected euer after, euen when he had framed his new fangled system of Philosophy and Diuinity altho he left scarce any footsteps of *S. Thomas's* Doctrin in either Being inuited to *Lisbo* to teach Diuinity in the English Colledge, he began to discouer some of those many errours which he then was hammering out, which coming to the Knowledg of the Inquisition, and his printed Conclusions being forbidden fearing the seuerity of that Tribunal he fled into England and was shortly after admitted into the *Chapter*.

The first remarkable Action I knew of him after this, was his Approbation of the booke *Deus, natura, Gratia:* A thing so odious

to

to the til' then orthodox Clergy, that at the next generall meeting Mr. *Broughton*, and seuerall others of the ablest refused to meet, unless he were remoued. To reestablish his credit, he printed some Controuersiall Dialogues, composed by Mr. *Rushworth*, whose name they bore: a treatise good in its self, yet he left the print of his foot in it by foisted errors namely that of *Scriptures being of no more vse to dispute , then a beetle is to cut with, or a straw to knock a nayl*: which R . S . Bishop of *Calcedon* deseruedly called *a Blasphemy*. Howeuer this and some others of the same nature past vnobserued amongst many good things contained in the book which buoyed vp his credit again, the book being attributed to him, and he either not at all, or but weakely disowning it

His next work was to strengthen himself in the Chapter, by introducing into it his disciples, who out of respect to their master, and Gratitude to their ben factors would stand to him, which succeeded euen beyond his own expectation for in a short time by the death of the ancient orthodox men, and numbers of other new ones, he became so powerfull in it , that nether the opposition of the Bishop , and his officers nor the censures of *Doway* first , and *Rome* afterward of his writings nor the dislike of the Catholicks nor the dreadfull death of seuerall of his Abettors without the Sacraments , a visible hand of God appearing against them , as Dr *Leybourn* truly sayd were able to put a stop to the Progres of his noueltys.

His temper was a deep melancholy which he encreased by his Continuall studyes . He had a good wit, yet clouded with a certain naturall obscurity, which accompanyed him in all his writings, which he found too tough an imperfection for him to ouercome , some think he affected it, that his sentiment not being Vnderstood might be more esteemed: others, that that might giue occasion of diuers interpretations of his meaning, and beget seuerall schooles, as there are seuerall jn *Aristotle*. In his Conuersation he affected a certain grauity or stoicall *Apathia* when he was amongst his admirers: but

when

when he met with ſuch as diſliked his doctrine, none more uiolent then he, as appeared by what he writ againſt Dr. Leybourn, my ſelf, Dr. Daniel, the Cardinals, and the Pope him ſelf, ſo he veriſyed his owne ſaying, *nec Divum parcimus ulli*: At laſt in a very great age, when he had outliued his greateſt diſciples, his Doctrine and his own vnderſtanding (he was grown a meer child again) he dyed as ſeuerall of his cheife diſciples had done, *ſine crux ſine lux*, without giuing any ſign of a Chriſtian. Which ſhall appear more at large in his life which I haue almoſt ready for the Preſſ

Doctor *Henry Holden* was as his own ſoul, for the vniformity of ſentiments: A ſun Diall doth not more exactly mark the motions of that Planet, then *Holden* repreſent the Doctrin of Mr. *Blacklo*. Beſides his title of Dr. of Diuinity of *Paris*, he had little to make him eſteemed. He neuer Could write ten lines of true *latin*: and his Phyloſophy and Diuinity were proportionall, yet his preſumption was ſo great that he thought none equall to him, except the all knowing *Blacklo*, as he vſed raſhly to call him, applying to that proud man one of Gods Attributes. He writ a booke called *Analyſis Fidei*, *Blacklo* haueing furniſht him with the materialls, and afterwards corrected the ſtile to ſalue *Priſcians* head lamentably broken in it to which he added a chapter concerning things in which Princes are to be obeyed, and in which they ought to be reſiſted. A tickliſh Point, and which required a greater moderation then his hot head was capable of in ſuch a dangerous coniucture of affayrs, when the People of England had cut off their king and kingſhip, and that of France ſeemed to deſign the ſame, if God had permitted it. So the chancellour of *France* cauſed the book to be examined; vvhich ſhortly after was burnt by the Hangman, and the Authour obliged to retract in an Aſſembly of the faculty of Diuinity, and would haue been baniſht *France*, had not Abbot Montagu interceeded for him.

This puniſhment would haue made another wiſe but not him for *naturam expellas furcâ licet vſque recurret*, Yet he meddled

dled no more with Temporal Princes for fear of their ſword; but ſpent his Pragmatical humour vpon the ſpiritual Superiour from whom he apprehended no ſuch danger. This appeares by his *letters* and *Inſtruction* for the Gouernment of the *Engliſh Catholicks* which , you will find hereafter.

R. S. late Biſhop of *Calcedon* vſed to ſay of him, that he was an *Vnlearned Preſumptuous raſh man*. His letters make good this Character.

A third was Sir *Kenelme Digby*, a man of parts deſeruing all eſteem, had they been accompanyed with Iudgment: of a great natural wit a tenacious memory a gracefull elocution, ſkilfull in many languages, and expreſſing him ſelf very well in ſeueral, but in Engliſh admirably, perhaps none before him and few after him more happily. This he knew and be ing aboue meaſure ambitious of honour he was eaſily wrought vpon to help to bolſter vp and ſpread the Atomical Phi-loſophy, which *Blacklo* perſwaded him would ſhortly preuail in the Chriſtian world, and baniſh Ariſtotle: which Honour they ſayd, he ſhould haue of founding this new doctrine, & diuinity it ſelf, which was to be new modeled alſo, accord-ing to theſe vnheard of Principles of that ſacred ſcience which till then had acknowledged no other then the Reuealed word of God and the Decrees of the Holy Church.

This conceipt of him ſelf engaged him in ſeueral ne gotia-tions of great conſequence in all which he miſcarried through lack of Iudgment in the managing of them. In ſo much as he was quickly forſaken by all who had employed him, *ſeque & ſua ſolûs amauit*: unleſſe perhaps Mr. *Blacklo* was a corriual in that loue: althô ſome with probability enough think his loue was rather *concupiſcentiæ* then *Amicitia*, rather grounded on intereſt, then any other quality: indeed in moſt of his letters we find *many* to be one ingredient, euen when Sir K. was at ſo low an ebbe of Fortune that it ſeemed to threa-ten his Bulging on the ſands.

The laſt Perſon, who furniſhes any conſiderable number of letters to this Collection is Mr. *Peter Fitton* vere *Biddulph*

of

of *Biddulph* in *Staffordſhire*, of a very ancient family. A man of competent learning, moderate, and truly orthodox: althô being made Preſident of the Engliſh Colledge in *Paris*, and Dean of the chapter, and obſeſſed by Mr. *Blacklo* and D. *Holden* he was ſo far wrought vpon by the importunity of the others, as to ground a ſuſpition, that for ſome time he ſided with the Faction *vltra fas*, *&* *las*, yet I hope he retained euen then his orthodox ſentiments, becauſe we find at that time Mr. *Blacklo* wiſhing he were *deromanized*, which ſhows he was not ſo: and he ſoon *renounced* all dealing with the affayres of that dogmatizing party, and retired to *Florence*, where he continued till his Dying day with an honorable Penſion from the Great Duke, who commended to him the care of his Medalles.

Some others are mentioned *en paßant* as Dr. *Georg Leybourn*, Mr. *Walter Montagu* Abbot of *Nantuil* in *Poietou*, Dr. *Humphrey Waring*, or Ellis, *Richard Rußel*, Biſhop of *Portlegre* in *Portugal*, &c. who being partly aliue partly very lately dead, are known enough to the greateſt part of our *Engliſh Catholicks*, *famâ bonâ* as is Mr. *Iohn Sergeant* alias *Holland*, *malâ*.

I publiſh theſe Letters out of the originals in their own hand writings, which for the ſatiſfaction of ſuch, as like S. *Thomas*, will beleiue nothing but what they ſee, I depoſited in the Engliſh Ieſuits Colledge at *Gant*, fearing the danger of beeing ſeiz'd on or loſt in *England*, ſhould I keep them by me. Thoſe who ſhall take the paines to viſit them, will ſee my Fidelity in following the originals, which I here preſent thee: as alſo that there are ſeuerall others of a much more odious nature, then any I here publiſh.

My earneſt requeſt is that what is here in contained odious, be n't attributed to the whole Body of the Clergy, vvhoſe honur is dearer to me, then my own life, but to the Blackloiſtical Party, under whoſe tyranny Orthodox men groan.

Some things I haue ſayd of this Party already in my *Letter de retinendâ Cleri Anglicani in ſedem Apoſtolicam obſeruantiâ*: ſome thing in *My Amuletum Excantationis*: more I will ſay in the life of his Patriark Mr. *White:* which is almoſt ready for the *Preſs.* Many things haue been ſayd by others, viZ Dr. *Leybourn,* Mr. *Coniers, Ionas Thamo,* and others, yet nothing ſeemes to bear ſo much of conuiction as theſe Letters: where in they ſpeak their minds them ſelues freely and deliuer ſuch ſentiments, which none would haue beleiued, with out ſuch an vndeniable euidence. Indeed theſe maxims althô contained in their other writings yet they are ſo obſcurely deliuered that they can not be clearly proued vpon them.

We ſhall ſee here that *Biſhop of* Calcedons authority which they pres ſo much againſt *Regulars* trampled on: the *Chapter,* which they recommend as canonical, to be with out any foundation or right to gouern, or giue Faculty: the oppoſition of Epiſcopal Authority when offred by his Holineſſ, ſo odiouſly charged on *Regulars,* owned to be their own Action, and laid at their own doors: that they are *Acephali,* haue *no Authority no ſuperiority no Gouernment no ſubordinaton.* In fine, *that they reſemble rather the confuſion of* Caluins *ſynagogue then the vnion of the* Catholick *Church:* as we ſhall ſee in the 14 Letter written by *Dr.* Holden, Aug. 30. 1647.

Which may ſuffice to excuſe my ſelf and ſuch other orthodox Clergy men as out of a principle of conſcience refuſe Obedience to thoſe to whome none is due, euen by their own confeſſions and acknowledgments: and who do not own facultyes, nor receiue Diſpenſations or Power to giue them, from ſuch, as certainly haue no Power at all. As alſo that ſuch Catholicks, as haue care of their ſouls, their greateſt concern, take heed of relying euen for ordinary abſolutions on them. whoſe Power is ſo diſputable, and vncertain, or certainly null. Read and Iudge, and pray for .
Thy harty well wiſher and ſeruant in CHRIST
Robert Pugh

Poſtſcript : Note that the greateſt part of theſe Letters came to my hands from Abbot Montagu whileſt I liued with or neer him: ſome very few were by him ſent to me after my retreat from his ſervice into a more laborious employment.

A Copy of a
LETTER
Of Mr. White to Dr. Holden.

Monſieur.

Though I had nothing from you this weeke, but a notaries Act, yet I muſt write vnto you. The occaſion is a word you writ to ſir Ken. that F. Hardiquan thanked you and that monſr Bernardiere was the cauſe. The which I wonder you ſhould write: for the effect being againſt the Queens intention, that is our ſtate for the preſent, you cannot haue deſerued thanks if you haue done according to her intention. The which neuertheles I ſuppoſe you haue done, both becauſe you haue taken the truſt vppon you, and becauſe you are none of thoſe, who think that priuate men vnder pretence of Religion may diſpoſe of Kingdomes, the which they doe who think that Ireland muſt be put in its own hands, and our King to rely vpon their faiths. For the Pope, or ſtrangers to order things ſo I eaſily conceaue it no inconuenience: But for an Engliſh man, I know not how he can do it with mantaining his duty to his country, that is, to God. God hath ſet diuers degrees in our country. and haueing giuen the charge of gouerning to ſome *eo ipſo* hath taken it from the reſt who are to promote their Religion all they can, vnder and not oppoſitely to the ſteerage of the common. This I write to be ſhewed to mr. Fitton whom when I was in Paris, I found vehement in that kind: and told him then as much, as I write now,

but

but feare I moued him not. Lett him conſider that if Ireland be made a ſouerain , both England and Ireland will be ruined temporally, and England by all probability alſo in Religion: for both will be engaged in a perpetuall war, and England hardened in hereſy by oppoſition, as we ſee it hath happed in Holland. But if the King for deſpayr , or neceſſity ſubmitt to the Parliament and all the forces of Scotland & England fal upon Ireland? If the good of Ireland be to keep England in war, are they Engliſh men, that ſhall ſecond this good of theirs? If I apprehend ryghtly , it is an eaſier matter to ſett England ryght , then to putt the Scots out of Ireland: This is to be don by ſieges of as ſtrong places as any be in Holland, that by a Feild, or two. England helped brings in Ireland: Ireland ſet vp makes the helping of England more hard . If Religion haue any footing in England, it will be miſtres in Ireland, but it may be miſtres in Ireland, and haue no footing in England. For loue of God be wiſe , and lett all helpes march together; for if one draw one way, and others other ways , all will be too little. And if all muſt go one way , it muſt be the Queenes way : for fittinger it is we ſhould ſubmit , then ſhee. you haue my ſentiment , and I ſhall be glad, if you do not like it at leſt that you ſhould know what conſtructions others make.

On the Back . Copy of *Mr. white* his Letter to *Dr. Holden* 29 May *All in* Sir Kenelmes *Hand.*   1645

Annotation . **What** *occaſion Dr. Holden gaue for this Letter , I cannot tell: certainly it muſt be of a very odious nature , otherwiſe the whole diſcourſe of this Letter is nothing to the purpoſe: probably Dr. Holden with his vſuall raſhneſſe gaue ſome adaice relating to Ireland , which diſpleaſed Mr. Blacklō , who was a Patriot euen vltra aras beyond Iuſtice and without due regard to ryght . Which appeared by his booke of obedience and Gouernment: where he pretends the King's ryght to his Crowne to ceaſe , when it cannot bee recouered* ***without***

without disturbance of the Commonalty. Preferring the Peace of a few cittisens before the iust ryght of his King, the Nobility, and a great part of Gentry who were at that time trampled vpon by the meanest of the Commons, in whose fauour he writ that book.

* * *

Sir. Ken. D. to Dr. Holden.

Sir,   *Epist. 2.*

I haue yours of the 3. currant: for which I humbly thank you. we neede not trouble our selues about the vncertanties, and disorders of our Letters, for now that commerce will be at an end: within two days after the next posts arriuall I hope to be gon hence, and then shall make all possible hast to you, possible to so many as I trauell with, 15. or 16. If you vnderstood my way of negociation, you could not dislike it: and to censure an important action, without knowing its principles, mr. Blacklow sayes tis french Leuity. Vpon occasion of your so mutch disliking what I do, I may without vanity say, that more is done for our good in this Court, then could haue been expected and it is enough to go thorough with our businesse: nor is it in their power, you mislike, to hinder it. And what is giuen to them is accounted thrown jnto the riuer, but necessary to make them propitious to permit the worke be done. *Cerberus* must haue *offam*, to lett *Æneas*, and other pious souls passe by him. But you will still Leap ouer the stile, *b*. before you are at it. Giue me leaue then to say, it were both honesty, and wisedome in those freinds you mention *c.*to forbear iugling vnder bord, to embroyl my businesses when peraduenture I work vppon the same principles, as they, and for many reasons know better then they, how to conduct it dextrously. But nothing serueth their turn,

It seemes that Sir. Kenelme himself, how true soeuer he were to the Blackloistical party, could not escape this man's censure

6. A true censure of Dr. Holden's precipitant way of proceeding in all things

that

. This complaint is well grounded.

d. This is a kind of Prophesy: for in reality it hapned as he foretells: as we shall see Letter 46.

e. A very ungratefull proceeding of Dr. Holden's freinds.

f. what he hoped for God knows; but it is certain he succeeded in no one point of his negociation, nether for the church, nor state: for he nether did the queen's businesse, nor the secular clergy's.

that is not don their own way. Remember what I say to you : d. At the end of my negociation, I shall be ruined (as much as the world can ruin me, which I valew not a strawv) for doing the iust contrary of what you tax me for. All in the mean time those from whom I shall expect the most correspondence, make my negociation vncomfortable to me by false biases, and foisted cardes. e. Since they once thought me fitt to be trusted with a businesse, they should haue relyed some what uppon my dexterity in the managing of it, who though I be no wise man, yet they know I am not a naturall foole. Neyther should they thinke it became me att euery time, and to euery person to reueale the secret springs I wrought by: they should be content to see it done to their minde in the end: and in the meane time permitt me some times, (without taking alarmes) to looke one way, whiles I rowed another. But the best is, I care not how any body taketh what I haue done, from the hyghest to the lowest; nor what becometh of me, whither applauded, or scorned. I am sure I haue done my duty honestly, and with some measure of **Prudence:** and God hath blest me with better successe, then at the beginning I could haue hoped: *f.* And I should haue yett had better, if these ouerwise sticklers for Religion would haue beene quiett, for by raysing diffidence, they haue made my conditions the harder, which is all well, if the King assent to them; but if we make him blanck at them, we ruine our businesse. And herein is the exercise of reason that giueth Iudgment, not onely vpon good appearing in one regarde; but *omnibus pensatis.* But enough of this. I hope to see you shortly.

On the backe: Part of my Letter to mr. Holden of the 25. 9 ber

1645.

secular clergy's. *He nether got a Bishop, nor the chapter confirmed. He disturbed all English residing in Rome, disordred all their negociations, troubled the ministers of* **that Court**, *Laboured to banish this man, and to affront that. And at last after much* *time,* tim, and mony fpent jn vain, with the queene's confent, he returned to *France*, leauing a bad opinion of his Perfon at *Rome* and bringing away with him a perfect hatred of the place and court: which he often expreſt in virulent termes to many, and was for that fharpely reprehended euen by moderate and ciuil proteſtants, jn Particular by my Lady Counteſſe of *Denbigh*.

❖❖❖❖❖❖❖❖❖❖❖❖❖❖❖❖❖❖❖❖❖❖❖❖❖❖❖❖❖❖❖❖❖❖❖

Moſt noble Sir.

The Parliament of *England* hath endeauored to fell fome men's eftates, but none vvill venture to buy them. It js thought they vvill giue a generall pardon, and fo get a round fum of mony by conpofition, fince that they cannot get jt by felling. I heare that the Scots hiue deliuered tnree querys to the Parliament. the firſt vvhether they jntend to depofe the King or no; The 2. vvhether they jntend to fettle the crovvn vppon the Prince. The 3. vvhat js the reafon that they do not eftablifh Church Gouernment according to the Couenant. The Scots jn *Ireland* are very vveak, and *Preſton* js novv entred jnto *Ulſter* vvith his army, hauing reduced all to *Conough*. This is the fum of our nevvs. And novv Iam called vppon to recommend vnto you our humble fuit concerning the chapter jn *England*. They cry out on all fides for vvant of fuperiors: *a.* and none can be made vntill the chapter be fetled. *6.* Thus vvith my vvonted refpects to your noble felfe I ceafe 21. fept.

a. Hence it appeares that none of any fide were fatisfyed with the fettlement of the Chap-

your moſt humble feruant
Peter Fitton.

on the backe from Mr. fitton 21. fept.   1646.

ter, otherwiſe they would not haue been on all fides fo clamorous for fuperiours, as hauing fome already. This we fhall fee confirmed jn the following Letters. Now *if the chapter from its begining was not canonicall, how could jt become fo after wards?* *Non firmatur tractu temporis, quod ab jnitio jure non fubſiſtit:* Is a Rule of the Law. *b.* The *b. The secular clergy may then set their harts at rest and be content neuer to haue any superiours, for jt js a folly to expect a Confirmation of their Chapter (without which there can be no superiours made) seeing the Chapter js so leauened with the Blacloist doctrine, and setled vpon such a foundation, in opposition to the Papal Authority, that it can neuer hope for any Confirmation thence.*

❖❖❖❖❖❖❖❖❖❖❖❖❖❖❖❖❖❖❖❖❖❖❖❖❖❖❖❖

Mr . VVhite to Sir Ken. D.

Most Hon : Sir.   *Epist . 4.*

This is only to acknowledge the honour you did me by yours of the last of sept . I think you will doe God good seruice, and the King also , jf you can gett the Pope to employ 40 - of our own sailes, *a.* for by good managing they will become a fleet for him, and Religion. If you can further procure that he should send such orders, or rather such a man jnto Ireland , that may conserue the peace , and seeke more after the substance then after the outside of Religion your Iourny will be well employed though you obtain no farther. As for my follyes, I sent you half the first part by Mr. Skinner : the second half goeth to back this . The Appendix had been ready also but that a pedler had more monyes then I, and soe a Catechism, that he had to sell at the next fair made my worke stay . *b.* I hope jt will be ready for my next Letters vnto you . soe with my best respects to your self , and your Coronel I rest this 25 . of october.

> Yours as euer to my power.
> Thomas White.

On the backe , from Mr . White 25 . october. 1646

a . Take notice here of the Pragmaticall spirit of this good man, who althô not called to it , must be giueing Directions to the Queene's ministers without, and probably contrary to her's and the King's orders.

b. There

b. There may haue been other motiues for that retardment that the Printer had fo much Learning as to fee that work contained Errors and fo much zeal as to be willing to take any pretence to delay its printing, althô thorough hopes of gain he was unwilling to Lay it quite afide.

❀❖❥❀❖❥❀❖❥❀❖❥❀❖❥❀❖❥❀❖❥❀❖❥❀❖❥❀❖❥❀❖❥❀❖❥❀❖❥❀❖❥❀

Mr. Fitton to Sir K. D.

Moft Noble Sir.   *Epift · 5.*

I Haue yours 19. nou. And your hopes of a good fucceffe in our bufineffe doth beget an affurance of it in Dr. *Holden*, and my felfe. As for our aduerfaryes they obie&ct the fame againft vs, which the *Parliament* obie&cteth againft *Bifhops in England*, and with as little reafon as they doe. And if poffibilityes of impertinencys may croffe the difcipline of the Church, there fhould be no Chapters, nor Bifhops in any part of the world: & if there be more fear of fuch impertinencyes in England, then in any other place, it is becaufe *a. Here he* we haue beene abridged of that authority, *a*. And fo per- *ownes that* aduenture may in the begining commit fome errours in the *our Englifh* managing of jt, but this danger will be the greater, the lon- *fecular clergy* ger we are depriued of that which we muft haue at laft and *know not how* the fooner we haue it, the fooner we fhall be acquainted *to vfe Epifco-* how to vfe it without committing the obie&cted impertinences. *pal authority,* Howfoeuer the fear of impertinences be it neuer fo great *if they had it* ought not to depriue vs of the thing it felf, but rather fuch *amongft them.* caution is to be vfed as may preuent the Impertinences, and *And jndeed jt* yet conferue the authority entire. I doubt not but you haue *appeared fo.* procured this already. And as for our bufineffes fince you *by the fucceffe* do fo kindly accept of the trouble, we fhall not acquaint *of the Late* any body with them, but your felf, when they are of im- *Bifhop,* portance, as this is, nether haue we acquainted Mr. *Skinner whom they* with this in particular, nor doth our clergy intend him *engaged jn*

*seuerall con-
trouersyes, to
the great
scandall of
catholicks
and no lesse
danger to
Religion.*

*b. This was
Mr. Iames
Skinner,
known to some
by the name of
Bently: a
uery orthodox
man, and no
freind to
Blacklos*

to be their Agent, although my Lord Bishop hath stiled him such jn his Letter to the Protectour: I suppose he meanes, that he js his Agent. Howsoeuer he expressed a great willingnesse when he went from hence to jndeauor to procure vs a pension, for our house here, and I could not refuse his curtesie, for I haue found jt that the discreetest men are not always the best beggers. But I leaue jt wholy to him self, to do what he pleaseth jn jt as holding jt desperate, yet foolish c. persons do some times preuaile jn this kind contrary to all expectation. Mr. White goeth to morrow from hence towards you he offered him self to assist vs jn procuring an English *Bishop*. we haue accepted of his curtesy with many thanks, when time shal require jt: but we jntend not to meddle jn that vntill this businesse of the *chapter* be ouer, nor then nether, vnlesse you do aduise vs to jt. f. you must charg Dr. Holden to send you French news, etc. 14. Dec. your most humble and faithfull seruant Peter Fitton. On the backe: from Mr fitton 14. Dec. 1646.

Noueltys; And for that reason gratefull to the Bishop of Calcedon, a profest enemy to them. c. By conuersing with Dr. Holden, something of his censorious spirit did work jn him: Other wise so moderate a man, as Mr. fitton would not haue thus censured Mr. skinner. d. This was Richard White Esquire elder Brother to Mr. Blacklo, who resided long jn Rome. e. Here we see, who they are that oppose the making of a Bishop: altho they odiously cry out on the Regular Clergy, as the only opposers of jt. It js the Chapter they seeke to get confirmed, and till that be done, will admit of no Bishop: and haue opposed a Bishop as often as he hath been offred, som times excepting against the Person, sometimes against his Authority, as contrary and consequently displeasing to the state. They are jnlued with some principles of Independantisme: vnwilling to obey, after they haue so long commanded, without controul of any.

f. This js the zeale for the Discipline of the Church and that Dignity establisht by Christ our Lord: which they by these words make to depend on the pleasure of a Lay man. No Bishop till the chapter be setled, that he may act nothing but what it shall appoint him. And no Bishop after that settlement, vnlesse sir Kenelme like of jt:

so

So here is giuen to Sir Kenelme Digby *an authority more then* Episcopal, *then* Archi Episcopal, *then* Patriarchal, *or euen* Papal: *all these being by the Institution of Christ bound to prouide Bishops, in due time where they are wanting; which here is left to the Determination of a Lay-man . Let the secular clergy boast as they please of their Endeauours to procure a Head to the English Church, & charg amongst their deluded disciples the Regulars with the odium of hindring it, neuer any Regular thought that grand affair So indifferent as to be left to the* Caprichio *of a priuat secularman, nor resolued to haue it stand, or fall by his* verdict.

❖❖❖❖❖❖❖❖❖❖❖❖❖❖❖❖❖❖❖❖❖❖❖❖❖❖❖❖❖❖❖❖❖❖❖

Dr. Holden. to Sir Kenelme Digby.

Sir .   *Epist . 6 .*

Mr. Fitton's arguments ought to preuail, if the *Pope* be head of the Church, but not otherwise, for then the next *Prouinciall Bishops* ought to prouide *Hereis aplea-* for their neyghbours. Adieu this 28. Of December 1646 . *sant condi-*
H. H. *tion put :* If
On the back in Sir K. D. Hand: from Dr. Holden 28 . the Pope be
December .   1646 . head of the
                                       Church ;
but not otherwise . *Is then the* Pope's being Head of the Church *brought to Iffs, & Ands? Is his supremacy become such a Topicke, as to be made to stand only as an Hypothesis by supposition, which way any impossibility may be sayd with Truth, as Sophists say of this other proposition: if a man flyes he hath wings. what shall we say to the* 2. *general Council, acknowledging the Pope to preside ouer the Fathers of it as the Head presides ouer its Parts? To the Council of* Florence *in which euen the Greeks acknowledged it. To that of* Trent *which expressely defined it? wither will these men Lead their Followers? vpon what quick sand will they build, haueing rejected the Rock? in what Cock-boat will they sayl, hauing abandoned the ship of S. Peter? To what flock will they ioin, who forsake that of* Christ.

most.

✦✦✧✦✧✦✧✦✧✦✧✦✧✦✧✦✧✦✧✦✧✦✧✦✧✦✧✦✧✦✧✦✧✦✧✦✧✦✦

Most honoured Sir.   *Epist.* 7·

I presume to enclose this in one to my Brother, though it
be an answer to yours of the 24. of Dec. because it bea-
reth nothing of hast. I desire you to consider that the notes
de Origine mundi are not a treatise, but an *appendix* added to
shew how Diuinity depends of Philosophy, & so hath all its
grounds in the former worke, without memory wherof it
is not well vnderstandable. I thought once to haue cited the
places of the Institution, but finding it would haue caused
some *brouillerie* with my printer, I easily declined to the sl ugh-
full side. Who shall consider, that nothing conformable to
nature hath hitherto beene deliuered of that subiect, will
require no ample discourses to make the Project probable.
For my expressions of your worth, they are far short of what
I desired, & could haue done afterwards. But I am a clod
of Earth, & feel my self gouerned by fitts & weathers, and
what I putt in my preface was the best that occured then.
As for Diuinity since the finishing of my Printing, partly
expectation of my Brother, and prouiding for him, partly
the weakenesse of my head, haue kept me from such con-
templations, and I feare will for some time. God knoweth what
is best. I send you the catalogue of some more errours then
are expressed in Print. I dare not say all, though the Printed
were enough to shame vs all, who had care of the Printing. God reward you for what you labour for the *Clergy*:
though I do not vnderstand why they desire it.

    Your most affectionate and humble Seruant·

                     Thomas White.

I pray vpon occasion presse my brother to Print.

On the backe *from* Mr. *White*; but no date. It seemes to
be an answer to Sir Kenelmes of the 24. Dec. 1646.
and so to haue beene written in Ian. 1647.

It feemes he regarded not in his Panegyrick of fr Kenelme, what his merits were, but what the Panegyrift could fay : for he doth not fay his words were proportioned to the obiect ; but to his own capacity. A pretty way of Prayfing indeed, in which much Sincerity is to be expected, when Reafon is fhut out of dores, & the only will confulted, yet if we confult the Practice of that party, and confider the Panegyricks they make of their own, and the inuectiues of Others, wefhallfind that Mr Blacklo is not the only, nor the cheife offender in that kind.

❖❖❖❖❖❖❖❖❖❖❖❖❖❖❖❖❖❖❖❖❖❖❖❖❖❖❖❖❖❖❖❖

Mr . Fitton to Sir K . D.

Paris 1. feb. 1646.

Moft noble Sir. *Epift.* 8.

I haue yours Ian . 7 And as for a *Bifhop*, I think it not conuenient to moue for one vntill our *Chapter* be confirmed, *a* . Which is of greater confequence. Nor then nether, vntil the times grow better, that we may haue wherewith to mantaine him. *b.*

a. Here is the reafon alleaded Letter 3. l. B.

On the backe : from Mr . Fitton 1 . Feb . 1647 .

b . Here is a nother reafon, why they would not haue a Bifhop : they haue not meanes to mantaine him : nor can haue, till times grow better. yet Bifhops are chiefly neceffary in time of Perfecution, in ill times, becaufe of the Sacrament of Confirmation, cheifely neceffary in thefe times : (ftill fuppofed that the Bifhops prefence be not caufe of the perfecution) as thefe fame perfons often fayd in defence of the Bifhop of Chalcedon . Now to refufe one lately vpon the fcore of lack of maintenance for him, is fo new in the Church, that I defy the whole party, to produce out of Ecclefiaficall Hyftory any one Prefident for it. And moreouer it is an affront to the body of Englifh Cathholicks to furmife them vnwilling to make him partaker of their Temporals, who Communicates vnto them fpiritual Graces .

I am

Mo*st noble Sir*.   *Epist*. 9.

I am glad to vnderſtand by yours feb. 18. That that buſie
man *a*. Is commanded to leaue the Citty. It is now no
ſecrete here, for F. Iohn writ it to F. Paul in theſe termes:
F. *Courtney is commanded by the Pope to retire himſelf to Liege, &
is baniſhed Rome, at Sir Kenelme his procurement by order from the
Queene of England.* Yeſterday I ſpoke to my Lord *Iermin* concerning him, & told him what I knew. Mr. *Grant* is now
diſpatched, & I hope he will ſettle all in Ireland; if Ormond
proue not falſe, that is, if he turne not Parlamentiere.
Mr. *Bennet* doth alſo returne back with particular inſtruction to my Lord *Digby*. As for your ſelf I haue giuen Mr.
Grant a note to remember to diſpoſe the Iriſh & the Nuncio
according to your deſire in your laſt Letter. The news
from *Ireland* are theſe: the generall Aſſembly ſits, but as yet
hath not publiſht any thing: they were at firſt diſunited by
the Marquis of *Ormond*, and *Clanrichards*, faction: but after
wards by meanes of the Nuncio they were vnited againe
Clanrichard is in *Dublin*, and hath declared himſelf for *Ormond*.
Where vpon rhe generall aſſembly ſent a body of horſe into
Gallaway to plunder all his Tenants, & adherents as they
did accordingly, only thoſe excepted, who tooke the oath
of *Aſſociation*, & now they are quartered vpon his Lands.
I am affrayde Mr. *Grant* will come too late to diſſwade *Ormond* from adhering to the Parliament, for *Ormond* writes in
his Letter to the Parliament they ſhould diſpatch ſuccours to
Dublin, with all ſpeede, becauſe he cannot hold out longer
then the 10. of March: in the meane time the Iriſh are
ſending both *Preſton* and *Oneale* to beſiege *Dublin* againe. I
vnderſtand now that Mr. *Bennet* his Iourny doth not hold,
and that my Lord *Digby* is sxpected ſhortly. Dr. *Holden* will
write vnto you how F. Paul beſtirrs himſelf againſt our *chapter*,
                                                              but

a. VVhat you may haue heard, and from whom, I cannot tell: but ſure I am that F. Courtny ſtayd in Rome *after Sir Kenelme's retreate thence and neuer left that place till his dying day*.

but I beleiue to little purpofe. He is affrayde that F. *Iohn*
b. will be fent after F. *Courtney*. Thus with my wonted *b* . *Father*
refpects I ceafe 15 . March.   Iohn   *neuer*
      Your moft humble feruant Peter Fitton. *ftirred out of*
On the backe. from Mr. Fitton 15 . March 1647 .   Rome: *fo Sir*
                                Kenelme

bad as ill fuccesse in procuring his banifhment , as that of F . Courtney.

✦✿✿✿✿✿✿✿✿✿✿✿✿✿✿✿✿✿✿✿✿✿✿✿✿✿✿✿✿

Mr. VVhite to Sir Ken. D.

Moft Noble Sir.   *Epift.* 10.

Thefe are to thanke you for yours of the 25 . Of march
and for the trouble *a*. you haue had for me. I am forry *a . This*
for your indifpofition, which I hope fummer will cure . I *trouble* *was*
pray thanke Sir *Michel Anzelo* when you fee him for his , & *occationed by*
tell him I intended not to deferue foe much honour as he *fome copyes of*
doth me. I pray remember mee alfoe to Monfieur *Bourgeois* Blacklow's
b. And monfr *Duchefne*. What you tell of metaphyficks is *Phylofophy*
a long winded bufineffe. I pray allfoe commend me to F. *which being*
Iohn Points his Prayers . *c* . I doubt not but you will eafily *fent to* Rome
anfwer the Fathers Authorityes, which they can bring, for *were feife d on*
there is none *d*. of which will come home . When you giue *by the*
me notice of S. *Bafil's* authority in particular, I fhall giue Inquifition,
you the beft account I can. But I feare it not *e* . My brother *which Sir*
hath written to mee, that my booke will not fell in Rome , Kenelme
becaufe of the opinion of the motion of the Earth. Soe *laba ured to*
that I may not trouble my felf with fending the 72 . dif- *retriue* .
ciples, vnleffe you can putt him in a better way, then he *b* . *Monfr*
knoweth any. I told him he muft get a ftationer there to Bourgeois
fend to his correfpondent here to take foe many bookes, *was the*
as he could vent eitheir vpon ready mony, or vpon a day. *Champion of*
                                               But

A Paper Composed by Dr Hart against Mr. Blacklo's Doctrin of the existence of Accidents without Subiect.

the Ianfenifts *in* France, *and fent to* Rome *to defend their* Errors, *c*. *You fee he was in* Charity *with one* Regular, *and thought his* Prayers *worth the asking*.

But he defpayreth of it. The Iefuits haue beene beaten here alfoe a little: but they will ftill fall on their leggs. My health hath beene foe doubtfull that I refolue as foone as I can gett mony to take fome waters, I beliue it will be about Iuly. In the meane while I reft this 18. Of April.

Your moft affectionate feruant.

Thomas White.

On the backe: from Mr. White 18. April 1646.

d. Thus he rafhly pronounces without knowing what was alleadged againft him e. with a like rafhneffe he fays, he feared not S. Bafils authority, altho he knew not what it was. The bufineffe then in dif-pute, blamed in Mr. Blacklo's Phylofophy, Was whither Accidents could fub-fift without a fubiect? The Chutch teaches, they can, this Mr. B. denyed. Againft him were produced 1. Council of Conftance, which in expreffe words con-demned that error, in Wiclef. 2. S. Bafil: As appeares by this following paper compofed by Dr. Hart, as the infcription on the, backe in Sir Kenelme's hand, proues.

✦✦✦✦✦✦✦✦✦✦✦✦✦✦✦✦✦✦✦✦✦✦✦✦✦✦✦✦✦✦

Teftimonium Concilij Conftantienfis et S. Bafilij. Quod accidens poffit exiftere abfque omni fubiecto

In Concilio Generali Conftantienfi Seff. 8. fub Anathe-matis interminatione prohibetur ōnibus et fingulis Catholicis ne de cætero 45. Articulos Wicleffi vel *eorum aliquem* audeant publice prædicare, dogmatizare, tenere velquomodo-libet allegare. Nifi ad eorum reprobationem:

Inter hos articulos: numero 2. hábetur: *Accidentia panis et vini non manent fine fubiecto in facramento Altaris.*

Et

Et ne quis dicat hanc censuram non vrgere, aut premere eos qui dixerunt *Impossibile esse Accidentia sine subiecto manere*: eo quod dicta Censura prolata sit sess. 8. quando nondum erat definita quæstio de Legitimo Pontifice Romano supremo totius ecclesiæ Catholicæ Capite, a cuius approbatione decreta Conciliorū firmitatem ac robur habent, sed lis pendebat inter Ioanem XXIII. Gregorium XII. et Benedictum XIII. quis eorum verus ac legitimus Pontifex esset: Sciunt omnes Martinum Quintum in eodem Concilio sess. 45. quæ est vltima prædictam Cænsurā ac damnatioem approbasse ut videre est in epistola dicti Martini; ad finem concilij.

Neque releuat si quis instet Concilium et Pontificem voluisse tantum reprobare Wiclefum, quod docuerit in Sacramento Altaris post Consecrationem sub speciebus panis et vini manere substantiam panis et uini: quod etiam intendit Lateranense sub Innocentio III. Cap. Firmiter. Tridentinum. Sess. 13. Can. 2. Et Textus. De Consecrat. D. 2. Cap. Species. etc. Nos autem. Vbi damnatur qui dixerit in Sacrosancto Eucharistiæ Sacrmēto rēanere substantiā panis et vini vna cum Corpore et Sanguine Christi : et negauerit conuersionem totius substantiæ panis et vini in Corpus et Sanguinem Domini manentibus dumtaxat speciebus panis et vini. Ex quibus non colligitur accidentia manere sine omni subiecto, sed solum non esse substantiam panis et vini, in qua, tanquam in subiecto recipiantur :

Hoc inquam, non releuat: nam Pontifex, et Concilium in dicto Constantiensi loco allegato distinguunt duos articulos Wicleffi : et 1. reprobant vnum quo dicit *Post Consecratio nem manere substantiam panis et vini:* Deinde reprobant alterū tanquam Articulum distinctum quo asserit: *Accidentia panis et Vini*

vini non manere fine fubiecto in Sacramento Altaris .

Atque hæc ex Concilio circa accidentium extra fubiectum exiftentiam in ffmo Euchariftiæ Sacramento. Vnde Conibricenfes expreffe dicunt effe conclufionem de fide , de quo Chriftiano Philofopho dubitare non licet , poffe deum confervare accidentia extra fubiectum .

Alia poffunt afferri teftimonia ad probandum accidentia poffe extra fubiectum exiftere ac confervari : Vnicum adducam ex S. Bafilio Hom . 6 . De Opere fex dierum. Vbi docet in primâ rerum creatione lucem folis productam fuiffe 1. mo die et manfiffe tribus diebus fine fubiecto ac tandem quarto die productum corpus folare, in eoque lucem illam primogeniam pofitam fuiffe.

Verba Auctoris funt : *Tunc* (id eft primo die) *ipfa natura Lucis producta eft : Nunc autem* (id eft quarto die) *hoc folis corpus conditum eft ut illi primogenita Luci vehiculum effet .* Hæc ille. Ac ne quis exiftimaret ipfum nomine Lucis intelligere aliquam fubftantiam Lucidam , non qualitatem accidetalem; Addit paulo poft : *incredibile nemini videatur & a fide obhorrens quod a me dictum eft : Aliud nimirum quiddam effe a luce fplendorem: aliud item corpus fubfidens Luci et fubiectum . Primum enim res omnes á nobis dividi folent in ipfam effentiam fufceptricem , et in eam quæ ipfi accidit qualitatem . Vt igitur diverfa funt natura, Albedo (inquam) et corpus dealbatum : fic et ea quæ modo diximus , differunt quidem , vnita tamen funt potentiâ Creatoris . Itaq, ne mihi dixeris fieri non poffe vt lux a corpore folis feparetur . Neq, enim ego huius a folis corpore feparationem mihi ac tibi poffibilem effe dico : Sed afferendum effe cenfeo , quæ mentis folius agitatione cogitationeq,* (fupple a nobis) *difparari a fe poffunt , ea reipfa feiungi facultate Creatoris vtriufq, natura poffe.*

Neque dicas S. Bafilium eo loco velle tantum Lucem folis differre a fole , ficut vis vftiva ignis differt ab eius fplendore , et poffe divinitus feparari , ita vt maneat fol abfque Luce : ficut fplendor ignis manere poteft in igne abfque eo

quod

quod vrat : deo (vt Scriptura loquitur) intercidente flammam . Aliud eſt autem ſolem exiſtere ſine Luce ; aliud Lucem ſolis exiſtere abſque ſole vel alio ſubiecto

Reſpondeo . Licet Baſilius hoc etiam ibidem aſſerat nimirum poſſe ſolem divinitus tantum ſeparari a luce , in quo diſtinguit ſolem a luna , quæ etiam naturaliter poteſt carere luce ; tamen aſſerit etiam aliud ; ſcilicet lucem ſolis tribus diebus manſiſſe extra corpus ſolis ſine omni ſubiecto , vt conſtat ex verbis paulo ante citatis .

Hoc teſtimonium Baſilij , magni faciendum eſt . Siquidem in concilio Florentino ſub Gregorio . IIII . Quæſtio circa S . Spiritus proceſſionem a Patre et Filio diſputabatur auctoritatibus SS . Patrum , et præſertim Baſilij vt videre eſt in diſputationibus Marci Epheſini et Provincialis Lumbardiæ a collatione 14 . ad vigeſimam . Præterea S . Thomas . 1 . p . q . 66 . a . 3 . Ait cælum Empireum non poſſe naturali ratione inveſtigari , ſed poni propter authoritatem Baſilij , Bedæ , et Strabi . Alia ad hanc rem de Baſilio dici poſſunt .

Ex his patet Wicleffum mentitum eſſe 2 . parte ſermonum , ſerm . 58 . Dum ait eſſe mendacium ſcandaloſum dicatque ante Innocentium III . nunquam auditum fuiſſe accidens extra ſubiectum eſſe nam Baſilius dixit inculcavitque accidens extra ſubiectum poſſe exiſtere , & extitiſſe . Floruit autem Baſilius ſub Valente Imp . Anno Chriſti 360 . Innocentius vero tertius anno . 1198 . Othone IV . Imperium tenente . Ex Genebrardo in Chronicis .

moſt

✣✤✥✤✥✤✥✤✥✤✥✤✥✤✥✤✥✤✥✤✥✤✥✤✥✤✥✤✥

Most Honoured Sir .   *Epiſt . 12.*

Theſe are to giue you accompt of the Iourney I intend to make, to wit firſt to the waters of *Pougues*, which are of vitriol. Thence I intend to ſee *Paris*, where if you pleaſe to command me any thing, I think the anſwers of theſe may find mee. From thence if the wars doe not hinder mee, I think to goe to *Douay*, whither the Preſident hath inuited mee to paſſ a uacation. Hee is a very able man, & all things conſidered peraduenture behind none of our Clergy. He accounteth himſelf extremely beholding to you, and imputeth it to mee, who am not as yet guilty, but if occaſion ſerue hereafter I ſhall be very glad to incurre any obligation for him. My intention is to ſee whither I can

a. You ſee how he Laboured to ſow Darnel amongſt the good Corne in that Feild. How far he preuailed I cannot tell. Dr. Hyde ſeconded his deſigne and countenanced his Labours; but he ſoon after dying,

plant any impreſſion *a.* of my doctrine in that colledge for I conceiue it may in time gett a great root, if it were ſett conſtantly on foot therein. Old Mr. *Smith* paſſed by, & the good old man gaue mee order to teſtify his great obligations to you very hartily, & both his company, & all others, who paſt heer giue extream good reports of your perſon. But they tell mee, that you would haue a care of my health, haue none of your own. Bee it for the greate paines you take, or as they thinke, that the ayre doth not agree with you. I Leaue here a picket of an hundred copyes to be ſent vnto you. The addreſſe is to your ſelfe, the recommendation to Mr. *Trichett* whom my brother and Signor *michael Angelo* both know. It is your goodneſſe, that is cauſe of your trouble. I doubt it will be a good while before they come. I pray lett Dr. *Bacon* hiue 4. which I promiſed him, & if my brother deſireth any, I muſt not deny him. Of your ſelf I ſay nothing, ſuppoſing you know you are maſter of all. Although I think you will not now
think

Think of remouing ſoe ſoon (theſe laſt news hauing ſet *Dr.*
new doubts vpon your affayres) yet I ſhall obſerue your *Leybourne*
order of leauing a bill at my Lodging, & at the Eſcu de *his ſucceſſour*
France. I haue no news, but only that *Plutark* de Placitis *weeded thoſe*
Philoſophorum L. 3. C. 17. attributeth my opinion *tares out.*
b. de *aſtu maris* to *Ariſtotle*, and *Galiſaus* to one *Saleucus* a *Amongſt the*
mathematician: which peraduenture will aſtoniſh your Ita- *venerable Fa-*
lians, who take them for new inuentions. Mr. *Bourgous thers, of the*
either is not yet paſſed, or at leaſt called not vpon mee. H. *Order of*
The *Ieſuits* it ſeemeth haue been to ſtrong for him euen in *S. Bennet,*
Paris c. No more but that I reſt this 4. Of Iuly. *he made one*
      Your moſt humble & affectionate frend & ſeruant. *Prſ lite, but*
                      Thomas White. *by the Autho-*
On the backe: from Mr. Blacklow 4. Iuly 1647. *rity of R.*
                                    F. Rudeſin

Barlow, *and the induſtry of* R . F . Stapleton, *then Profeſſor of Phyloſophy, &*
ſince Dr . *of Diuinity & worthy Preſident general of the whole congregation that*
one man was remoued, & that doctrine quite baniſht your houſe. b . *It is no news*
to any, who are conuerſant in the workes of ancient Authours, that Blacklo's *opinions*
ſhould be found in them: for they will find them all in thoſe workes: Blacklo *only*
reuiuing antiquated errors, which he expoſes as of his own inuentions, ſuppreſſing
the Authours, from whom he borrowed, or ſtole them. Now he mentions thoſe, whence
he tooke that de Æſtu maris *to ſtop the mouths of the* Italians, *who accuſed it*
of Nouelty .
    c . *It is no great wonder that in the town of* Paris *ſo Orthodox & zelous*
for the Faith of their Anceſtors, monſr Bourgeois, *who defended all the Errours*
of Ianſeniſts, *and* Arnauld, *in his booke of* Frequent Communion, *ſhould*
be worſted. He had many ſupporters, & very powerfull Patrones; but Magna ve-
ritas & preualet. *And the* Ieſuits *hauing in that controuerſy Truth, & the God*
of Truth, & the Church, which is the Pillar of Truth on their ſide, might eaſily
ouercome him .

❀❀❀❀❀❀❀❀❀❀❀❀❀❀❀❀❀❀❀❀❀❀❀❀❀❀❀❀❀❀❀❀❀❀

Moſt noble Sir .   *Epiſt . 13 .*

I haue yours Aug. 5 . And I am glad that our buſineſſe
is in way towards an end : & I do not wonder that monſig-
neur *Albize* , & Padre *Hilarione* plead againſt vs , being men
alltogether ignorant of the ſtate of our country , & who
neuer had their eare s open to any but to our Enemys . I
wonder more at *P . Luca* : but when I conſider , that he is a

a. A pretty. *Fryer , a* . he may be excuſed . That which doth moſt aſto-
ſturre on that niſh is the weakeneſſ of their motiues . As firſt that they
whole Holy ſhould call this an innouation in the Church , I am ſure it
order . is not , & for vs in particular it hath been practiſed amongſt
vs theſe 25 . yeares . As for the 2 . it is no wonder
if they repented ſtill the Gouernment they gaue vs , for they
b. Yet they neuer gaue vs any *b* . that was canonicall , as this is . As for
had giuen them the 3 . if they pleaſe they may chang the title of *Calcedon* ,
two Biſhops. and call him the *Biſhop of England:* for my part I ſee no inconuenience in it . Howſoeuer the Pope may erect our
c. Here againe Chapter , *c* . and giue vs a *Biſhop* , when he thinks it expedient .
the Chapter is The 4 . is of little force , for not withſtanding Card. *Millinos*
vrged ; & the actiueneſſe in procuring ſuch denials from the congregation ,
Biſhop I am ſure the congregation did neuer intimate to vs any
poſtponed . order to ſuppreſſe our Chapter , or any miſlike *d* . of it
5 . if they are fryghted to offend the Engliſh Regulars , they
d. His Holi- haue no reaſon to diſcontent the Clergy , who I am ſure
neſſe and the will in the end be more able *e* . to do that court ſeruice , or
congregation diſſeruice then the Regulars can be . And laſtly whereas they
haue always apprehend danger of making *f* . a Patriark it is ſo chil-
expreſt a miſ- diſh , that I know not what to ſay to it : but if any thing
like of the can put vs vpon ſuch courſes certainly it muſt be when
Chapter . we find by Experience , no hope of obtaining from that
court any requeſt we make , be it neuer ſo iuſt . Yet after
all this I cannot diſpaire of a good ſucceſſe of our buſineſſe ,

as long as I consider that our Protecteur, & your self are
Actors in it, & so I will passe from it to a matter that concernes vs more neerely.

    You must know that at last not only the *Independents*,
g. but the *King* himself do giue vs solid hopes of a liberty
of conscience for *Catholicks* in *England* in case that we can but
giue security, that our subiection to the Pope shall bring
no preiudice to our allegiance towards his Maiesty or that
state: it is true the King will not appear in it; but would haue
the Army to make it their request vnto him: & so I vnderstand he hath admited the Catholicks to treate with the
army about it.

    The businesse will be to frame an oath of Allegiance
(for this it is which the army requireth of vs) & I beleiue
we shall do it without aduice from that court, for we haue
found by experience so little successe there in any businesse
that tends to the good of Catholick Religion, if it be not
ioined with their interests there, who proceede vpon principles of Policy, & are oftentimes guided by factious persons,
as that we haue little encouragement to hazard the embroyl-
ing of a businesse of concernement by putting it in to their
hands before it be fully finished. Howsoeuer you may do
well to see if you can discouer any vnderhand dealing in
that court concerning that businesse, for I doubt not but
that the *Iesuits*, and *Benedictins* there will be tampering vnderhand about it, yet I can assure you they will haue little
to do with it in *England.* *h.* You may also of your self take occasion to try the pulse of that court, & see how they will relish
it if we declare that the doctrine of deposing Princes is
no article of faith. To which I suppose, Monsig. *Albizi*
will reply 1. That we are hereticks. 2. That we will nether
preach, teach, nor persuade that doctrine. 3. That we will
discouer all such as shall preach, teach, or persuade it. 4.
That in case the Pope should actually free subiects from
their allegiance in England, *k.* we will renounce any such
discharge from him. Some such thing as this I suppose
will

e. He is ne-
ther a Prophet
nor son of a
Prophet.

f. Before long
we shall see
them nibling
at that very
thing, or some
thing worse.

g. Here be-
gins the treat-
ing with the
Independants.
of which
much here-
after.

h. This
cleares Regu-
lars from the
blame of de-
aling with
those Rebels,
& charges it
on the secular
clergy, & the
chapter Party.

i. nether monfigneur Albizi, nor any can think, the Depofing Power to be an article of Faith: & fo could not call any Hereticks for denying it.

will be done, if we cannot get it at a cheaper rate : & fo you may do well to difpofe that court to it, but without taking notice as if any fuch thing were actualy on foot; but only by fuppofing to his Holineffe & others that you conceiue the *Independents* will in conclufin exact fome fuch thing as this from vs. You may alfo make aduantage of this bufineffe to get fome thing from the Pope to oblige the Queen, & to keepe the King in a good mind towards vs. Ireland is in a poor cafe &c. Thus with my wonted refpects I ceafe 30. Aug.

Your moft humble & faithfull Seruant
Peter Fitton.

On the back : from Mr Fitton 30. Aug. 1647.

k. This all Catholickes, euen Regulars fubiects to his Maiefty, will readily figne.

❖❖❖❖❖❖❖❖❖❖❖❖❖❖❖❖❖❖❖❖❖❖❖❖❖❖❖❖❖❖

Letter of Dr. Holden to Sir K. D. in French

Monfieur *Epift.* 14.

* Here is a compendium of the three ftates of Fråce brought on the ftage to Iudge of Clergy's gouernment in England. A Bifhop for the clergy : A

Ayant veu celle que vous auéz pris la peine d'efcrire a Monfieur Fitton, & me trouuant a diné chez * vn Prefident de mes amis de cette ville, ou il y auoit vn Euefqne & vn Docteur de noftre faculté, & leur faifant raport des peines que vous prennés d'obtenir l'eftabliffement de quelque authorité chretienne & canonique en Angleterre, ilz fe mirent tous a vous louer, & dirent des merueilles de vos beaux talents. Car vous eftes cognu de prefque tous ceux quy eftoyent a table. Et comme Ie leurs ay conté quil y a plus de vingt ans de ma cognoiffame quil y a en Angleterre plus de fix cent pretres feculiers, & trois au quatre cent Religieux, & beaucoup de milliers des Catholiques laiques, &

tout

tout cela fans Euefque, fans authorité, fans fuperiorité, fans Prefident fubordination, fans gouuernement, *a.* chacun dit, chacun fait ce qu'il luy plaift, viuants pelle melle fans ordre, & fans regime & qu'auec toutes les fupplications, & toutes les folicitations, que nous auons peu faire en court de *Rome*, pour auoir quelque authorité, & quelque Iurifdiction canonique nous n'auons Iamais fçeu rien obtenir, & que vous meme y trouuéz des difficultés infuperables. Le Prefident dit en cholere tout haut, *b. Ces bougres d'Athées veullent ilz encore perdre ce peu qui refte de Religion en Angleterre? nous fommes heureux de n'eftre fuiets au maudites maximes de cefte court fimonique & infame.* Et le Prelat me diti *Monfieur vous deuéz vous addreffer au Clergè de France, c.* ayant prealablement faitrefoudre la queftion en forbonne, que cela fe peut, & fe doit faire. *a.* Ie vous affeure, Monfieur, cette Procedée dela Court de *Rome* fait crier vangeançe a tout le monde, & ruine l'authorite Papalle. C'eft peu de chofes quela confirmation de noftre *d.* chapitre, vous nous deuez faire donner quatre ou çing *e.* euefquestitulairs du Pais, que pourroyent gouuerner leurs Eglifes felon l'inftitution de Iefus Chrift, & l'ordre du droit. Ie fuis refolu de voir ce qui dira noftre faculté a cefte queftion, que Ie vous enuoye cy iointe, car iamais il ny auoit tant d'apparence de liberté pour les Catholiques en Angleterre qu'afteure, & il eft par trop infupportable de viure toufiours foubs vn ioug fi pefant, & dans vn defordre fi effroyable: nous refemblons pluftoft ala confufion du fynagoge de *Caluin*, (*deeft aliquid*) a l'vnion de l'Eglife Catholique. *f.* En fin vous fçauéz que *extremis malis extrema remedia*, ce que vous ne pouués effectuer a *Rome*, I'efpere le faire a *Paris*, ou Ie feray en attendant voftre retour, plus que Iamais

    Monfieur votre tres humble & tres affectioné feruiteur

                      Holden

De Paris ce 30. Aouft 1647.

for the nobility, & the Doctor for the third state. No wonder, that the Poet, who difpofes the farce fhould make them fay, what he pleafe.

a. This is falfe: for within thofe twenty yeares there were two Bifhops: the later was then actually aliue, & had his vicar Generall, in England: befides other fubordinate offices. And the Chapter was then in Being: whofe authority they recommended to thofe who depend on

                On

On the back : from Dr. Holden (in French) 30 Aug. 1647.

them, at the ſame time, that in corners they own it to be nothing . b . The caſe hauing been ſo ill ſtated, no greate wonder the Gentleman ſhould diſlike the Proceedings . Yet ſuch words as theſe reliſh more of Dr . Holden's ſpirit & paſſionate heate then of a Preſident of the Parlament of Paris . Here is an embrio of ſchiſme which the faction hath euer ſince beene licking into ſome ſhape . d . The confirmation of ſuch a Chapter as that of England is of ſo vaſt conſequence, that it can neuer be hoped for by any wiſe man . e . How vnconſtant theſe men are in their deſires . Sometimes no Biſhop, till they can mantain him ; now nothing but four or fiue will content them : ſometimes they ſolicite them from France ; now Sir Kenelme muſt procure them from Rome : ſometimes they muſt haue titles in Partibus ; now their titles muſt be Engliſh . And ſtill clamors againſt Rome for not condeſcending to euery requeſt, whileſt theſe men blame to day what they demanded earneſtly yeſterday, & will to morrow condemne, what they ſolicite for to day : proceeding with their ſpirituall ſuperiours, the Pope, as the ſectarys at the ſame-time did with their Temporall ſuperiour, the King Petitioning for what they pleaſe, & reſolued before hand to be diſſatiſſyed with the Anſwer, whither it were a Grant, or a Refuſall .

*   f . How the ſecular clergy will like this deſcription of their ſtate from one of their cheife Brethren, I cannot tell : but ſhould any Regular haue made it, he would haue heard of it with both his eares .*

*   g . He was deceiued in his expectation : for nether Rome nor Paris thought conuenient to grant ſuch a fauour to ſuch a body of men .*

❦❦❦❦❦❦❦❦❦❦❦❦❦❦❦❦❦❦❦❦❦❦❦❦❦❦❦

A Queſtion to be propoſed to the Sorbon.

a . The Barbariſmes, & ſoleciſmes contained in this writing, ſhew its   Quæritur an ſuppoſito quod ſumus Pontifex reſpueret vel negligeret Catholicos Angliæ, 1 . e . numeroſo fidelium Anglorum gregi Epiſcopos prouidere, quodque iam per multorum annorum ſpacium exhibitis in hunc finem ſedi Apoſtolicæ infinitis propemodum ſupplicationibus, & variorum preſtitis nunciorum ſollicitationibus, dirâ conſtaret experientia, liceat ne fexcentum & amplius Sacerdotibus fæcu laribus, & millium aliquot Catholicis Laicis omni fuperio- ritate iurifdictione *b.* Regimine privatis vicinos Galliarum Epifcopos appellare, ac deprecari, vt iuxta Conciliorum & Canonum decreta, acephalis fibi, ac perturbatis & incompofitis Epifcopos providere dignentur.

    Hanc ego proponam quæftionem facultati noftræ, cui haud ignoro quam mihi datura refponfionem, Nempe appellationem licitam effe, & Epifcopos *Normanniæ* tanquam vicinioris provinciæ poffe ac teneri iure Canonico, & charitatis præcepto acephalis hifce, & incompofitis Presbiterorum & fidelium Laicorum numerofis turmis Epifcopos providere.

    Hoc facile præftabit, cum fæpius fele obtulerit *Archiepifcopus d. Rhotomagenfis.* Effectum verò fuftentabit parliamentum *e. Angliæ.* Quibus fi quis reftiterit, non Religionis; fed factionis caufa puniendum, & ablegandum effe iudicabitur.

Authour, who could neuer write fiue Lines without, them, as thofe who knew him very well afure.

b. Let the ficular clergy take notice what opinion this man had of their Bifhop, & Chapter, to which they exact obedience from others. c.

Onthe Backe: Dr Holden's queftion with his Letter of the 30. Aug. 1647.

The concealing of the Anfwer of the faculty if the queftion was euer propofed, & that no effect followed it, fhews that it was far different, from what he promift himfelfe fo confidently. d. His Grace neuer would do any fuch thing: he was cleare-fyghted enough to fee the confequence of fuch an attempt, fo contrary to the Practice of the Church. e. He reckned without his hoft here: the Parliment's intentions were far from fo much kindneffe for any Bifhops, or Papifts, fufficiently appeared by the following perfecutions in which the fecular Clergy, notwithftanding their humble Applications to it, found little more fauour, then the Regulars, who did not bend their knees to that Baal

    f. Catholicks may here fee, what meeke men they are like to find the Blackloift faction, if they get Power, or credit with thofe who haue it. Here is Punifhment, and Banifhment, defigned for all, who fhould not haue acknowledged that illegall, & vncanonicall Gouernment. And to bereaue thofe Catholicks

Catholicks of the Comfort of suffring for their Conscience, (althõ that alone should moue :h m to refuse to adore those Idols) they should be banisht not for Religion but for Faction. VVhich is so fit a description of what Catholicks haue of late suffred, that we may think the contriuers of the Persecution took their Idea from this man. VVhich coniecture will be more confirmed, out of Larger explication of this design, in Dr. Holden's Instruction.

❖❖❖❖❖❖❖❖❖❖❖❖❖❖❖❖❖❖❖❖❖❖❖❖❖❖❖❖❖❖❖❖

Dr. Holden to Sir Kenelme Digby Resident for the Queen of Great Brittany at Rome 6. of Sept. 1647.

Sir   *Epist.* 16.

a. It could scarce be in a stranger stile, then this is.

I haue yours of the 12. of the last which came to me a week too late, for had it come before I sent you my Latin Question, & my French Letter, I should sure haue written in a strang stile. *a.* Vppon the Proposition of an Oath of Allegiance in *England* Mr. VVhite, i. e. *Blacklow*, & I met at Mr. *Fitton's* to whom we proposd the Oath of the Dialogue or discours you mention : but he like a *Roman* could not digest it : we stood so strongly for the Iustice of the cause, that we declared no less should be offred, & so nothing is don. In the interim in England my Lord *Brudenall* the cheife Actor with the Army in this businesse, and who consults only with Iesuits, & Mr. *Montagu* whose zeal & phansy is stronger then his knowledg in this case, hauing discussed the businesse, & maturely considered all things, are sending or haue sent to *Rome*, for his *Holinesse*

b. Very elegant, acute, and witty. *b. Bulls* to beget *English Calues*. I am so mad at them, that I am going back to my hermitage, that I may hear of such fooles, and *factious fellows c.* no more. I hope to be 15 days absent

absent, & by that time I hope my choller will be appeafed. I could find in my hart to go ftreyght to the Independents Army, and make them demand d. what either the Catholicks fhould perform, or els be banifht for Traitors; not for Religion. And the very truth is, Sir, that could I perfwade my felf the Independents would fettle the Kingdome, I would haue been in England ere this, I fhould either vnite the foolifh Catholicks, e. or hang them; but I can not imagin that England muft be fetled f. thus. The Prefbiterians may make head, the Independants may be diuided, & many other things may be which I fore fee not, I can only confeffe my ignorance. Mr Fitton will be more carefull of his correfpondence hereafter, but I would haue you come away, vnleffe you can get a fubfiftance there, for our Clergy is not worthy g. the paines you take for them: nor will neuer dare go to the clofe ftool without a Breue from Rome. I told you in my laft, I wifhed you in England, there you myght do good indeed, & if euer the Catholicks haue wit to make themfelues confiderable, now is the time. But Prefton in Ireland & Sir Iohn Canffeld in Rome will neuer work g. miracles. I fuppofe its Dr. Leybourne h. puts Canffeld on. I was going about to reprint the dialogue with the Petition, & Proteftation of Fidelity, but there's no good to be don where the Inftruments haue fuch maleuolous, or malignant influences into a bufineffe. There's no mony to be got any where, nether out of England, nor in France. Here's a letter from your fon as I beleiue. The fecrets fintiers dellamour de Dieu, fhall be bought becaufe this is the third time you haue written for them. Here's Mr. Fitton's Letter which will tell you all news. A dieu this 6. of September.

In right margin:
e. Thefe Noble men are much obliged to him, for his charaŝter of them.

d. He prefumes very much on his credit with the Independants.

e. More difcouerys of his kindneffe to Catholicks: before he would haue them banifht; now hanged: if they did not fubmit to his dictamens. It is well the Curfed cow had fhort hornes.

On the backe, in Sir Kenelme's hand. From Doctor J. Holden. 6. Of Sept. 1647.

In right margin:
This vnfetled condition of the

Nation faued the Catholicks from the ftorm, with which this bluftring man threatened them

them . The Clergy is much obliged to you , for your honourable opinion of them.
g . I neuer heard of any that Dr . Holden wrought vnleſſe it were that writing,
& talking at the rate we ſee here , none ſhould haue returned his civilitys in ſome
way proportionable . h . Dr . Leybourn is very much in the books of the Blackloiſts:
we ſhall hereafter find it ; & haue occaſion to wonder they ſhould treat in ſuch a
manner a worthy man , & a Brother .

❀❀❀❀❀❀❀❀❀❀❀❀❀❀❀❀❀❀❀❀❀❀❀❀❀❀❀❀❀❀❀❀

Mr . Fitton to Sir K . D.

Most Noble Sir   *Epiſt.* 17.

Ihaue yours of Aug . 19 . And as for our buſineſſe I doe
now in a manner giue it ouer for deſperate . The truth of
it is I do wonder at that court, & I do not vnderſtand it,
if we would make as little account of our duty towards
that court, as they do of Iuſtice towards vs, I aſſure you
we haue at this preſent an occaſion offred vs to giue them
as deep a wound, as they do vs , if we will but ioin with
the *Independents a.* & vſe their aſſiſtance , to vindicate our
ſ.lues ; & yet we need to do no more, then what ſhall be
moſt iuſtifiable in conſcience . Beſides I am certain at this
preſent that if we will , it is in our power to thruſt the Ieſuits *b .* out of England. What we ſhall do, or attempt I know
not , only this you may aſſure his Hol. That if what we
haue ſo long deſired be now at laſt denyed vs, I beleiue
we ſhall haue little commerce *c .* hereafter with that court:
but relying uppon the Iuſtice of our cauſe , we ſhall ſeek
to redreſſe our ſelues the beſt way we can , & I hope we
ſh.ll not be blamed, if we chance to ſet certaine queſtions
on foot *d .* which the Diuines on this ſide of the Alpes do
hold may be diſputed without breach of vnity of the Church.
But now to other buſineſſe . The propoſition of the oath
goeth on

a . It ſeemes
all of that
gang had
great Conſi
dence in the
kindneſſe of
the Rebels .

b . It ſeemes
the Ieſuits
were not ſo
much in the
fauour of
thoſe Rebels .

goeth on *e* . & feuerall ones are already framed by vs . If his *and 1 eafily* Hol. chance to take it ill that we doe not aduertife him , *beleiue]-l it.* of what we are doing in this kind , as I fuppofe the *Iefuits*, *Yet 1 fhall* & others do , you may tell him , that we haue no encour- *nether enqui-* agement to deal with that court in any thing , confidering *re what in-* how they haue dealt with vs vpon all occafions euer fince *troduced the* the beginning of this fchifme . Howfoeuer let him not feare fecular Cler that we fhall do any thing , but what fhall be approued of gy , *nor ex-* by Learned & Catholick *Diuines* . *f.* *cluded the*

Regular

My Lord Brion is newly com out of Ireland &c .

I am your moft humble feruant Peter Fitton . *from that*

fauour.

On the backe . From Mr . Fitton 13 . Sept . 1647 .

e . *To deny*
communication , *or commerce with any Perfon or Church* , *was the old forme of Excomunication; & when betwixt two churches it was a fchifm . This is threatned here becaufe he fays they refolued to haue little commerce with Rome : not declared becaufe they would retain fome . How confcionable this is I need not to fay , much leffe hom far from Piety . The hing fpeakes of it felfe .*

D . Hinc illæ Lachrimæ . *This is the root of all thofe Exotick opinions concerning* Purgatory, Indulgences, the Pope's Authority , *the* Oaths , &c ,*which haue been fet on foot* , *& afferted with great boldneffe by the* Secular Clergy *of late* , *& almoft euer fince this time . I wifh all who hear them aduance fuch* Noueltys, *knew* , *that when they plead for their truth all their reafons are* Non caufa pro caufâ : *for the tru & only reafon is that they are offended with the* Pope : *& doe not intend to affert a Truth; but to fatiffy their Paffion . e* . *This is a* Flea *put in his Holineffe eare* , *with defign to allarme him : Yet I neuer heard his* H . *was moued there with .*

f . *I eafily beliene Mr. Fitton was really perfwaded of what he here writes other-wife he wouldhaue detefted the whole, for which he pleads, whofe perfons he Loued ; but much more the* Church . *Yet certainly the fequele hath proued , that there was ground to fear they would teach fuch doctrines , as no Catholick Diuine euer taught* Viz , *that of* Purgatory . Catholick Doctrine *is like an* Arch *of which each part hath both a connexion with , & a dependance on all the reft : & no one can be remoued without the fall of the whole, nor loofned, without fhaking all . I am perfwaded*

that

that scarce any of the Heresiarkes *foresaw all the Errors, they breached at last: they thought onely some particular Truth, which they thought salvâ Fidei Compage, myght be denyed. Then by naturall consequence they were brought to question other Points, till little was left vnstirred. So seditious men seldome propose open Rebellion, & a totall dissolution of the Gouernment, at the begining of their commotions. They design to be free from some inconuenience, eased of some burthen, redressed in some either real or pretended wrong: but when they are once engaged, they know not how to withdraw, nor where to stop, & so are perswaded to perseuere, & defend one seditious Action by another.*

❧❧❧❧❧❧❧❧❧❧❧❧❧❧❧❧❧❧❧❧❧❧❧❧❧❧❧❧

Dr. Holden to Sir K. D.

13. 7ber 1647.

Sir.   *Epist.* 18.

a. Marke the
opinion this
good man
hath of the
Catholicks of
the whole
Nation.

b. The busi-
nesse, he
speakes of, &
desires he had
neglected,
other he had

I thought to haue been in my solitude ere this, but I haue differred it vntill munday Labouring to think of some meanes how to free our *foolish English* Catholicks *a.* not only from losing that liberty which they were neuer in such hopes of since Queene *Mary's* days, but from that ruin, which they will run into for want of a little wit, or knowledge. Had you been in these parts some weekes a goe that you myght be in *London* now whateuer become of businesse, *b.* you would easily haue layd such grounds, as that an vnspeakable good to *Catholicks* would follow in time, though not presently. And truly could I perswade my self that the *Independants* would be able to settle the state, I would be in *London* within 10. days. I suppose Mr. *Fitton* will tell you that now Mr. *Haggerston* is dead, Mr. *Brudenell* the elder, Mr. *Smith*, &c, are our Agents sent down to the Army. I cannot read with patience the Letters our friends write. My former to you will
fitt

fitt the ſubiect you write of to Mr. *Fitton*, & if the *Inde-pendants* doe continue to ſecond vs I feare not but *Rome* will content vs, if not we ſhall find ſatiſfaction elſe where. *c.* I here ſend you a ſheete, *d.* I haue cauſed to be printed, whereof I haue ſent ſome copyes into *England* with thoſe *Inſtructions* in writing which I here ſend you alſo, you know how ſecret all this muſt be. Theſe I haue ſent will I hope come to *Parliament men's* hands. I conceiue you may freely giue out the *Independants e.* intend vs an abſolute tolleration, & that they declare themſelues already, & that they will let *Catholicks* haue their *Biſhops*, & the rather to counterpoint the *Proteſtant Biſhops*, &-therefore deſire they may be titular of the Kingdome : that leſſe then ſix will not be ſufficient in *England*. Which if you make any ſtay there, & that the *Independants* goe, & that the Pope will doe what he cannot refuſe, or what at leaſt muſt be don without him, I ſhall eaſily ſpecify here after the *Biſhopricks* which are to be de-ſired, *f.* with the ſhires of other *Biſhoprickes*, which are to be annexed vnto them de preſenti with the names of thoſe, who are fitteſt to be promoted. This you ſee I haue already complotted the whole buſines in my *idle Brain*. But as ſoon as I get into the foreſt of *Beaumont*, I ſhall forget all theſe thoughts. I haue gott *les ſecrets ſentiers* &c, but the *Anatomia Animæ* is not to be found here. I ſhould wiſh you to gett ſuch a *Breue* as you gott for *Madame de Chamberge*, that is le-aue to enter into the monaſtery of *Saint Marie au Fauxbourg* ſome times a year with one companion for *Domina Lucia de-la Roche foucault vidua Domini de Touraille*, *Domina adhonores Illuſtriſſimæ Principis de Condè*, &c. But I feare it will not be worth the labour : it is Mrs *Mა. Gerbier* puts me on. What will become of her two ſiſters, I cannot tell you as yet. Here's one from *England*, I know not from whom. I would you, & I were both of vs there, though I know not as yet what effect the beſt endeauours would haue. *Iohn Lee* is newly come to *London*, & he hath vndon me by his too long abſence.

I feare

---

vndertaken them, were thoſe of the King, & Kingdome, recommended to him, by the Queene, which he then promoted (with what earneſtneſſe is eaſily ima-gined) in Rome.

c. They build very much vppon their Credit with Indepen-dants which what a quick-ſand it was, did appeare ſoon.

d. This ſheete neuer fell into my hands : ſo what it con-tained I know not. But the *In-*ſtructions *follow this Letter.*

I feare that *Frere*, & *Bee* the booke binders will cofen me of Mr. VVhite's bookes, becaufe *Iohn Lee* was fo long abfent, & the bookes were out of my hands, before I knew that they make difficultyes to pay me. Here's one from your Son. I am iuft now called vpon to goe into the town & therefore Adieu.

e¹. By the effects we may gueffe at the intention of the Inde pendants better then by their words.

Yours as euer H. H.

13. 7ber 1647.

On the backe: from Dr. Holden. 13 Of 7ber 1647.

f. Here the good man takes vpon him by Authority Patriarcha', *& Hyper-Patriarkal to difpofe the whole Gouernment of the* Catholicks *to name Bifhops, affigne them their* Refidences, *diuide their* Diocefes prefcribe their *limits, determin their Authority, & reftraine their Power. By whofe Commiffion doth he this?*
g. It feemes the heat of his zeale is like a ftraw fire it quickly vanifhs otherwife a Iourny of three houres riding could not blot all thefe thoughts out of his mind. VVhether thefe tranfports were an effect of Paffion, *or zeal, let others gueffe. Their vnconftancy fhews them very imperfect.*

❀❀❀❀❀❀❀❀❀❀❀❀❀❀❀❀❀❀❀❀❀❀❀❀❀❀❀❀❀❀❀❀❀

Dr. Holden's Instructions.

If it fhall pleafe the Parliament to fuffer the Roman Catholicks to liue amongft them with liberty, & freedome lett it likewife pleafe them to take this aduice from a Roman Catholick for their greater & better fecurity.

First Let no foreigne King or ftate intercede for them, nor meddle in the compounding of bufineffes for Catholicks; but let the Catholicks fee the Parliament giues them freedome meerely out of their own difpofition, and good will towards them.

a. By what Authority

Secondly *a*. Lett this Oath fent her with in print be vniuerfally taken by all Catholicks of what profeffion foeuer

euer. And if there fhall be found any one Ecclefiafticall or Secular, Religious or Lay who fhould refufe it Let him be defired to withdraw himfelf out of the Kingdom as an vnfit member of the Common wealth, as things now ftand. Thirdly let the Catholicks haue, or rather oblige them to haue fix or eyght Bifhops more or leffe by whom they may be gouerned. Lett the Bifhops be titulars of the Kingdom, caufeirg them to renounce, expreffely by Oath all rents, reuenues, & temporalityes belonging to thofe Bifhops. By the firft part of this claufe thefe Bifhops will be fufficiently *Independent b.* of the Pope, which otherwife they cannot be; & by the fecond all fufpition of pretending to or hindring from the difpofall of thofe Bifhopricks, or Bifhops eftates will be taken away.

Thefe Bifhops will be (as all other ordinary Bifhops are) in the beleife of all Catholicks *fucceffors to the Apoftles,* hauirg authority immediatly *c.* from *Chrift Iefus* himfelf, & confequently *independant* of all other *fpirituall power,* euen of the *Pope* himfelf. For though all *Bifhops* are bound to acknowledge the *Pope their head or the cheife Paftor,* yet he cannot impofe any fpeciall command vpon them of what nature foeuer vnleffe both they, & the common wealth in which they liue doe think it fit. And this hath been the practice heretofore in Catholicke times in *England,* is now in *France,* & in all other *Catholicke ftates & Kingdomes.*

Let all clergy or Ecclefiafticall men, be they fecular or Regular depend *d.* on thefe Bifhops, & make them renounce *d.* all immediate dependence of any other whomfoeuer out of the Kingdom. And this becaufe diuers Regulars pretend to be exempted by the Pope from all ordinary Epifcopall power, & Iurifdiction & to be immediatly fubiect to the Pope, or the Generall of their order n, & of a forrain nation. Wherefore lett all *Priefts* both *fecular & Regular* take an *Oath,* & oblige themfelues thereby not to exercife any *Ecclefafticall Function,* or any *fpirituall authority,* or Iurifdiction

doth he propofe this Oath, vnder paine of Banifhment?

b. How can hauing titles in the Kingdome, make them Independant on Rome, feing all Bifhops heretofore were dependant, altho titulars in it?

c. Can yours, or the Parliaments nomination make their Authority, be immediatly receiued from Chrift, & not the nomination of the Pope?

d. *Here is a nother iniunction contrary to the Canons of the Catho-lick Church, impoſed vnder pain of Baniſhment.*

e. *VVhere did Chriſt ordain, that all Lay Catholicks be ſubieſt to Biſhops not canoni-cally made ; but nominated by ſuch a Pragmatical Man, as this is? & con-firmed by a Rebellious Parliament?*

f. *VVhat Law can oblige a Biſhop to anſwer for all the Crimes of his Chiefs,*

Iuriſdiſtion, but by the leaue & as deriued from the ſayd Biſhops. Which whoſoeuer ſhal withſtand, or ſhal pretend to depend immediatly of any foreign Prelat or power what-ſoeuer, lett him, or them be wiſhed to withdraw themſelues out of the Kingdom, as vnfit members of the common wealth, as now things ſtand.

A'l the lay Catholicks of the Kingdom (accordling to the beleife of all Catholickes) will be truly, & by *Chriſt's* inſtitution *e.* ſubieſt to theſe *Biſhops* in all ſpirituall things, & conſequently theſe *Biſhops* may be in ſome ſort made an-ſwerable *f.* for all their *ſubieſts* Crimes (if any ſhould happen) againſt the ſtate. And Leaſt theſe *Biſhops* ſhould extend their ſpirituall authority *g.* too far eſpecially in things, which haue relation to the *Temporall Gouernment* as in *probats of wills*, dif-poſall of *pious Legacyes*, iudgments of *marrages* &c, It will be ealy to limit their *Iuriſdiſtion* in theſe occations as it may be thought fitt in the diſcuſſion of particulars·

Now becauſe *h.* the Ieſuits doe ſeem to be the moſt dangerous body, & are thought to be moſt faſtious by all Chriſtian ſtates not Catholicke, if they, or any other Re-gular Order refuſe either the Oath here with ſent in print, or to be ſubieſt to theſe Biſhops as before, lett them bee thought vnfit members of the common wealth, as now things ſtand, & therefore lett them be wiſhed to withdraw them-ſelues out of the Kingdom, not for their *Religion. i*, But for the ſuſpition the ſtate may haue of them, which the reſt of the *Catholickes* will not oppoſe, *k.* no more then they did in venice, & other Catholicke ſtates, much leſſe in a Kingdom not Catholicke.

On the back : Doſtor Holdens inſtruſtions into England ſent me with his Letter of the 13. 7ber 1647.

vnleſſe they are chargeable on him, for hauing commanded, counſelled, or abetted them, or that they are Committed through his negligence of his function? what

Country

Country euer called Bishops, or any other superiours to account for the faults of their subiects, except on those scores?

g. Here he takes vpon him to restrain that spiritual Authority of the Bishops, which before he taught was independant of the Pope, & not restrainable by him. For he takes to himself, & giues the Parliament a greater power ouer them, then he ownes in the Pope the head of the Church. So his Power is Hyper-Papal.

h. Mr. Fitton in his Letter of this day speakes of an admirable aduantage they had ouer the Iesuits, & that it was in their power to thrust them out of England. (See Letter 16.) & Dr. Holden very charitably proposes it to the Parliament. But the Parliament had other busines to think on, then this: & by slighting these malitious suggestions, shewed more discretion, then to follow or regard such Ignes Fatuos.

i. Here we haue another hint at such a persecution, as Catholicks suffer at present, not for Religion, says the Gazet; but for the state, & the suspition it may haue of them. Suppose after the Iesuits, the Clergy should be vnder a like pretext banisht? Is it not possible it may in a like manner giue suspition to the state? Hath it not effectually don so, euen in Catholick times? VVhat Policy is here, to dig a pit for another, into which they themselues may as well fall?

k. Catholicks. who haue a care of their souls will not willingly part with Regulars as long as they see the secular Clergy promote so many erroneous dogma's contrary to Faith, & these schismaticall principles contrary to Charity.

VVere this scribler a liue, I should desire to know of him, by whose commission he makes this addresse to the Parliament? It containes things concerning all the Catholicks of England, it imports the design of an Ecclesiasticall Gouernment vnheard of in the Christian world from Christ's time till this day, & all imposed with so great a penalty as Banishment, had he an Order from Catholicks to offer it? Had he their aduice? Did he so much as communicate it to them, or the maior, & chiefer part of them? Not one word of that. VVhat doth this rashnesse deserue in a priuate man, to deal such busines of so general concern of his own head?

Addistion to these notes: Is there not reason to suspect, that this design did not dye with Dr. Holden; but Liue still in that party? & that Mr. Sergeant's great design in his going for England, is this same.

If

✦✦✦✦✦✦✦✦✦✦✦✦✦✦✦✦✦✦✦✦✦✦✦✦✦✦✦✦✦✦

If it fhall pleafe the Parliament to fuffer the Roman Catholickes to liue with the fame freedom & enioy the fame
liberty which the other free borne fubiects of the Kingdom
do, & which their naturall birth ryght feemes to challeng
as due vnto them Let it pleafe them to take into their confideration thefe few heads propofed vnto them by a Roman Catholicke, who knowing the principles & maximes of
the Roman Church, & beleife, conceiueth them fit to be
thought of, for their better fatiffaction, & greater fecurity
of the ftate.

First let no forrain King, nor ftate be fuffred to
interceede or medle in the behalf of Catholicks, to the end
the Catholicks may fee their freedone doth only proceed
from the Parliaments gratious difpofition & willingneffe to
fettle vniuerfall liberty, & confequently that they are not to
depend, nor hope, nor be obliged to none but them for
their freedone.

2ly, that fuch an Oath of Allegiance be framed
(if it be thought neceffary that any be requifite) as may
ftand with the principles of Catholick Religion (whereof
there is a draught in Print will be eafily made fully fatif-
factory) which may be vniuerfally taken by all Catholickes
of what profeffion foeuer, & if any either Ecclefiafticall, or
Lay fhould refufe it, let him be banifhed out of the Kingdome, *a*. as an vnfit member of the Connon wealth.

*a. Here Ba-
nifhment
is cleerely
commanded
in cafe any
prefume not to
conforme
to his*

3ly. Let the Catholickes be obliged to haue fix or
eyght Bifhops more or leffe, by whom they may be gouerned in matter of Religion & confcience. Let thefe Bifhops haue fone of the ancient nationall titles of the Kingdome according to their feuerall diftricts, & confequently
haue ordinary iurifdiction ouer the Catholicks. By thefe meanes, that is for as much, as thefe Bifhops haue nationall
titles

titles, & confequently are *ordinaryes* (as we call them) the
Parliament is fecured, the Pope can hiue no Power ouer
them to the preiudice of the ftate. For they being *ordinaryes*
he cannot depriue them of, nor limite nor touch their Iurifdiction at all; being a generall tenet amongft Catholickes
that all *Ordinaryes* are fucceffours to the Apoftles, & hiue
their authority immediatly from Iefus Chrift, & confeqiently
as innouable, & abfolute in their kind, as the Popes in
his So that all immediate influence from the Pope vpon the
Catholickes of England is cut of by this meanes, & therefore no fear of the Popes arbitrary power, which can be
only fufpected, & dangerous to the ftate. Thefe *Ordinaryes*
will gouerne the confciences, & fouls of their flocks by their
owne proper authority, which we hold to be innate into
their offices & perfons *Iurediuino*. Hence it follows that thefe
Ordinaryes are not bound to obey or receiue any fpeciall
command from the Pope of what nature foeuer, if either
contrary to the cuftomes, or canons of the Church or preiudiciall to the temporall laws, & gouernment of the ftate,
whereof the ftate it felf is to be iudge. It is tru thefe *Or-*
dinaryes muft acknowledge the Pope the firft Bifhop, & head
b. of the Church; but not receiue any of his commands
without the leaue of the ftate. Whereupon thefe two generall tenets may be exacted of thefe Ordinaryes, & of all
Ecclefiafticall, & lay Catholicks of the Kingdome. *First that*
no Catholicke of what profeffion foeuer fhall acknowledge any forrain,
or outlandish authority, or superiour either Pope, or other ouer his
person, or personall actions in any ciuil or temporall practise, or busines
whatsoeuer. Secondly that no act of command, or authority either spi-
rituall, or temporall from the Pope, or any other outlandish person of
what quality foeuer fhall be receiued, or admitted by any Catholicke
of what condition foeuer, without the knowledge, & confent
of the ciuill magiftrate.

4ly Where as thefe *Ordinaryes* aboue mentioned,
who may & ought to oblige themfelues not to receiue any
com

the iniunc-
tions: *which*
in the other
Instructiõs
was expreffed
more sweetly,
Let them
be desired
to withdraw
out of the
Kingdome.
But the sense
in both is
the same.

b. Here is a
new kind of
head, with-
out any au-
thority, or
Influence
ouer its Body.
A thing mon-
strous in Na-
turall, &
much more in
mysticall
bodyes.

commands or orders from the Pope as aboue, without leaue from the ciuill magistrates (which hath been the practise heretofore in Catholicke times in England is in now in France, & all other states & Kingdomes) whereas I say these *Ordinaryes* might seeme by reason of their titles, to giue suspition of their pretension to the temporalityes of the Bishoprickes where of they should beare the titles, (which connot be iustly suspected) the lands being sold by order of Parliament yet may they be obliged by oath to renounce all claim & title to the lands, liueings, or temporalityes of those Bishoprickes vnder what pretence soeuer.

5ly where as feuerall forts of Regulars or Religious are sent from the Pope to exercise Pastorall functions, & guide the Consciences of lay Catholicks who pretend to be exempted by the Pope from all ordinary Episcopall power & iurisdiction, & to be immediatly subiect to the Pope himselfe, or to the Generall of their order in, & of a forraine country, lett all such & all other Ecclesiasticall & clergy men whatsoeuer oblige themselues by oath to depend immediately on the aforsayd *Ordinaryes*, as they ought to do by the canons of the Church, & not to exercise any Ecclesiasticall function, or spirituall iurisdiction but by the leaue, & as deriued & receiued immediatly from the sayd *Ordinaryes*. Nor shall any pretend to haue any spirituall power, or faculty immediatly from the Pope in any either spirituall, or temporall affaire whatsoeuer, or from any other outlandish person whatsoeuer, saue only from the aboue mentioned *Ordinaryes*, or their officers natiues of England. Which whosoeuer shall refuse, or withstand, or will pretend to depend immediately of any forrain Prelat, or Power lett him be banished out of the state.

6ly. Where as the lay Catholicks of the Kingdom will be subiect in matter of Religion & conscience to these *Ordinaryes*, who are their tru & lawfull Pastours (according to the doctrine of the Catholicke Church) & this by Christ's institution

inſtitution, & expreſſe command (as all Catholickes do beleiue) & are therefore anſverable for ſoules: & farther are obliged both by the principles of their Religion, & by their particular intereſts to be watchfull ouer the perſons, & actions of the Preiſts whom they appoint vnder them, to guide the conſciences of the layety; It will be of no ſmall ſecurity to the ſtate to admoniſh, & charge theſe *Ordinaryes* to be vigilant. & carefull, that nothing be complotted, nor attempted againſt the ſtate, & to diſcouer it if they ſuſpect or hear of any ſuch thing, they being in ſome ſort anſwerable to the ſtate for ſuch crimes, as may be committed by their ſubiect. againſt the temporall power, or Gouernment through their negligence, or conniuence, either by the Preiſts, whom they appoint, or by any of the Catholick Layty.

7ly leaſt theſe Biſhops ſhould extend their authority too far, eſpecially in ſpirituall things, which haue a neer relation to the temporall Gouernment, as in probats of wills, diſpoſall of legacyes, Iudgment of marriages, &c, it will be eaſy to limit their iuriſdiction in theſe occations, as the ſtate ſhll think fit in the diſcuſſion of theſe particulars.

8ly. If any Catholick Eccleſiaſticall, or ſecular, or Regular ſhll refuſe to ſubmit to theſe *c.* particulars, lett them be *c. Thus this* baniſhed out of the ſtate, as vnfit members of the common *Dictator* wealth: the ſtate declaring their baniſhment not to be for *enacts laws,* their Religion, but for the ſuſpicion it hath of their loyalty, *with ſeuere* whereat other Catholickes can take no exception, no more *Penaltys,* then they did at the expulſion of the Ieſuits out of the ſtate *which our* of Venice, & elſwhere, nay much leſſe conſidering a ſtate *nation neuer* not Catholick hath more reaſon to be cautious, & wary *owned the* of ſuch perſons, then a Catholick ſtate hath. *King himſelf*

Beſides theſe generall heads, *d.* wherein many par- *could do, but* ticulars are comprehended, which would require ſeuerall diſ- *in Palia-* cuſſions & reſolutions, there be many other particulars, *ment.* which are to be referred to thoſe who treat, & agitate this buſineſſ with order, & Commiſſion.

As

d. Haueing determined by his owne head the substantiall points, he leaues some circumstances to be discussed by the body of Catholicks, when the generall heads require greater discussion, & more mature deliberation then the particulars.

a. VVhat a rash, & vnheard of Proposition, is this: that an Hereticall assembly of Rebels can inuest ordinary Priests with here-tical Autho-

As to what is to be don in case the Pope refuse to giue Bishops to the Catholickes vppon these termes, conceiuing twill exclude his power out of the state, & preiudice the greatnesse of his Court by giuing such a president to other states to do the like, whether in case of refusall the Clergy & Layty may not haue recours to France, or Ireland to haue Bishops from thence? & whether some Preifts may not be appointed in the interim, whose power by the state's assistance may be Equiualenr *e*. to this in effect?

Whether these Bishops should not make knowne to the state the places of their ordinary abcad?

Whether the clergy should not make known to the state both at the first, & afterwards from time to time the names, & persons of those whom they choose to be Bishops, to the end that none be promoted: against whom the state may haue any iust exception?

How, & in what manner the Catholickes may haue their Assemblyes of Diuine seruice, for number places. &c?

What habits their Bishops, & Priests may wear openly?

Whether & how the Catholickes may be admitted to any publicke charg? or bear any office in the common wealth?

What cours is fit to be suffred for the education of Catholickes Children in Learning, or other qualityes, that they may not be sent ouer Sea to bee brought vp amongst forraines & strangers, mantained vpon the Pope's & other Princes pensions which draw many inconueniencyes into their dispositions.

No writing vpon the back, till of late about 3 Yeares agoe: but is all in Dr. Holden's hand writing.

rity equiualent to that of Lawfull ordinary Bishops? *VVhat opinion had he of the* Authority of Bishops *who aduances this? Yet this man must be thought the Asserter of* Epscopal Authority?

Nate

Note, that there is a copy of Inſtructions *in Mr.* Fitton's *hand, blotted & interlined, ſo as it ſeemes to be the firſt rough draught of them. But the penaltyes annexed to non conforming Catholickes are blotted out, yet ſo as they may ſtill be read. I think this attempt of one or two priuate men to preſcribe Laws to the whole nation A raſh Preſumption, not to be paralelled by any in ſacred or Prophane Hyſtory.*

❖❖❖❖❖❖❖❖❖❖❖❖❖❖❖❖❖❖❖❖❖❖❖❖❖❖❖❖❖❖❖❖❖❖

Mr. Blacklovv to Sir K. D.

Moſt Hond Sir   **Epiſt. 21.**

Theſe are to humbly thank you for yours of the 29. of Iuly: which I receiued at Paris, & to giue you accompt of my returne to Lyons. The wars about Doway hindred mee from going thither, & ſoe miſſed of my mark yet I hope I haue done ſome good at Paris As for the buſineſſe of Ireland, by ſome diſcourſe with Mr. Bennet I perceiue that Marqueſſe Ormond had truly a deſigne to keep low, if not ruin Catholick Religion by ſetting a diuiſion betwixt the nobility & Clergy, he ſupporting the Nobility to ruin the Clergy. Alſoe that Owen Oneale is a man both of wit, & martiall ſkill. I am ſorry you are ſoe greatly troubled with the Clergyes buſineſſ, the which I wiſh to goe well *a.* cheifely becauſe you are engaged in it. My waters would haue don well with mee, had I not been fixed on my Iourny, which cauſed me rather to ſtay, then take them. See I ſtayed 10. days: yet I conceiue thus much refreſhed my body. I am not yet ſoe ſkillfull in my diſeaſe, as to be able to giue a good account of it, & therefore ſpake but in common to Dr. Fludd of it I am glad you take that courſe with obiections of Phyloſophy & Diuinity, to examin them Ioint by Ioint: for that will carry you thoroughall: but am ſorrie you are importuned in the kind. I ſhall be glad, & humbly thank

a. A very zealous man, for the Clergy, who regards leſſe, how their general concern goes, then for the Perſonal concern of Sir Kenelme I

i   **you**

b. The King is much obliged to this man who thinks, he doth scarce deserue, that for his seruice Sir Kenelme should hazard his. health!

you for what soeuer you shall doe, for M . *Hyle.* I shall be sorrie you should venter there another winter, with so troublesome health *Vix Priamus tanti b.* God send your businesse done in good time, that you bee not putt againe to a winter Iourney. At my coming from *Paris* I found a letter from Mr. *Chanron* of *Grenoble*, in which he says he can giue you satisfaction concerning the *Mercury* of *Saturn* I intend to send him word, that he bee very well assured of it, & for the rest I shall expect your order. There is growing a businelT, wherein peraduenture you will be importuned, concerning an *Oath*, the which *Catholicks* should take to haue the penall laws renuersed. But I hope it will not stay you there. For neither doe I apprehend this present state will stand, nor that any thing will bee done in *Rome* concerning such a subiect, with that expedition or rationality as is necessary for our affaires: neither that there is the place to treate such a businesse which importeth the *circumcizing* of *Papall Authority*. I had not the honour to see your son *George* at *Paris*, for while I was at S. *Germans* his vacation came in & he was sent into the Country. Mrs. *Mary Capland* it seemeth hath found the way to apply *Mathematicall abstractions* to *materia sensibilis*, which I feare her master will be long a doeing. I am here out of news, the which I doubt not but these times dayly afford you store of: wherefore I rest as euer. Lyons Septem. 19.

    Your most affectionate & obliged freind & seruant.

                Thomas White.

On the back: from Mr. White 19. Sept. 1647.

✿✿✿✿ ✿✿✿✿ ✿✿✿✿✿✿✿✿ ✿✿✿✿✿ ✿✿✿✿✿✿✿✿✿✿✿✿✿✿

Sir Ken D to Sir Iohn VVintour.

                    Rome 30. 7ber 1647.
                           Sir

Sir *Epiſt.* 22.

Till yours of the 5. Aug. (which I conceiue you miſtake
for *September*) I had not heard of your 4. weekes abſence,
& therefore was in pain at your long ſilence. My buſineſſe
here would allow me the like, for I haue nothing to write
to you about. But my reſpect will not ſee you remaine long
vntroubled by me. Yet too I haue a word to ſay vnto you,
concerning F. *Courtney* : *a*. He is hugely mortifyed, & afflicted
that you ſhould haue ſhewed my Long letter concerning his
ſubmiſſion to the Queen, vnto ſome body in *Paris*, that
hath written hither to his Generall out of it things extreamely
to his preiudice. But I bad him reſt ſecure on that hand, for
that I knew your prudence ſo well, & your vnderſtanding,
ſo entirely what belongeth to a Princes ſecretary, that you
neuer ſhewed to any body Letters of ſecret aduice that concerne the Queenes ſeruice, & much leſſe ſuch as myght
blaſt thoſe whom the Queen receiues into her graces & is
pleaſed to make vſe of vpon occaſions. This comforted him
a little, but withall I was faine to go to his Generall yeſterday to do him good offices there : for vpon his return
to her maieſtys ſeruice, all thoſe who were formerly his declared freinds, & ſupporters, are now his violent *b*. enemys;
& will in the end remoue him with mortification from
hence, *c*. if her maieſty avow not powerfully her protection
of him, which as things ſtand in this court, & particularly
with him, is moſt for her ſeruice that ſhe do. Therefore if
any thing be broken out in your quarters to his preiudice
from my letter, I pray you ſilence it the beſt you can. The
late defeate of *Ireland* maketh all *Kinuccinis* freinds, & moſt
of this court hang the head. They now repent the breach of
the peace with my Lord Ormond. In fine, they are much
miſtaken, who expect any good from this court, otherwiſe
then meerely for their owne intereſts. Therefore our Engliſh
Catholicks

a. See on the
other ſide the
Annotation. a.

b. This is
moſt malici-
ous againſt
the whole
Court of
Rome, as
repreſenting
it to be full
of moſt bitter
enemyes to the
Queen which
is not only

false, but incredible also & the easy acceptance of Sir Kenelme's intercession for F. Courtney proues the cōtrary.
c. This predi-ction is as false as the relation: they neuer did remoue F. Courtney.
d. VVhat follows is conformabe to

Catholicks are very simple, *d.* that treat here any allowance of what they are transacting with the Army in *England.* Let them guide themselues by what is in it self iust, & fit: for if they introduce this court into the treaty, they shall be cosened, & the businesse will be foyled vnlesse it be managed wholy in pursuance of their ends: & then I am sure it will be very auerse to ours. For they care no more for what *Catholicks* suffer in *England,* then the *Marechal de Gramont* or my Lord *Powis, e.* or other such good natured men, doe care for what the Christians suffer in *China,* or *Iapan.* God send us once wise, & to stand vpon our leggs. We shall then be vpon good termes, with God, our Prince, our country, & all good, & wise men in the world though peraduenture this court (not the Church) of Rome will scold at vs. I pray you see my Letter to my Lord Iermin, & I rest.

Your most humble & faithfull seruant

Kenelme Digby.

On the back: To Sir John Wintour 30. Sept. 1647.

Blacklo's spirit false, rash, & tending to schisme. e. A great & groundlesse reproach to those noble men: who being parts of the mysticall body of Christ, cannot but be sensible of what it suffers any where.

Here we haue a tale of a tub, without sense, reason, or Probability: F. Courtney to be banisht, & yet stayd there: the motiue of his banishment, his submission to the Queene's orders, & Deuotion to her seruice; yet stopt, & the sentence reuersed vpon a word spoken in her name. All his freinds changed into bitter enemys, because he promoted her concernes; & changed again to be his freinds, because they were told her Concernes required it. VVhat a sicke man's dreame doth this greate wit relate, being awake!

VVhat is certain is, that Sir Kenelme going to Rome as the Queenes Minister, vndertooke the businesse of the secular Clergy, which he thought required the remouall from that place of all such as were not well affected to it, such as he thought were F. Courtney, & F. John, the one of the Society, the other a Benedictin. In this he thought to haue preuailed once, as appeares by Mr. Fitton's

Letter

Letter of the 15. *of March of this yeare.* (*vide lit.* 9.) It is now no secret here, for F. John writ it. *He knew it therefore before, thô as a secret. And probably to procure it, he had vsed her* Maiesty's *name, thô doubtlesse without her order. At last finding his negociation fruitlesse,* (F. Courtney *being too well knowne, & feared in that Court, to be remoued vpon such friuolous reasons, as were alleadged against him*) *to saue his owne credit, he pretends,* F. Courtney *was conuerted to the* Queene's *seruice* (*to which he neuer was auerse althô he had been represented otherwise by her Minister to her*) *& that it was necessary for her seruice, he should be taken into her protection, & was stopt in* Rome *by his interest. Thus he colours the ill successe of that vndertaking, & when he was really foyled, proclaimes himself victorious, as the vnlearned* Pretender *to* Learning *doth in* Lucian.

❀❀❀❀❀❀❀❀❀❀❀❀❀❀❀❀❀❀❀❀❀❀❀❀❀❀❀❀❀❀❀

Sir Ken. D. to Mr. *Fitton*

Rome 30. 7ber 1647.

Mosthonoured Sir   *Epist.* 23.

I humbly thank you for yours of the 6. cadent. And am ryght glad to heare of so good disposition of the *Independants* **a.** towards vs. For Gods cause let vs not forfeit it by tampering indiscreetly with this court, to limit our dutyes to the *King*, & *state*. In such cases they consider not vs, but their owne sordid ends. It is a shame to see how deafe they are to true charity & piety, **b.** & how eagle eyed to their owne temporall emoluments. Some good men here say it hath not bin always thus in this court, in so extreame a degree. But that it is your zealous frend *Innocent* & his tender conscienced Sister-in-law, that haue brought all things to their own bias; according to the old law, *Regis ad exemplum totus*

I hear the Pope hath already been written vnto in the name of the *English Catholicks* about what they haue in agitation

with

a. Of this good disposition we neuer had any reall effects.

b. A very Charitable representation of the Persons in Rome.

with the army. But I cannot beleiue it, much leſſe, that Mr. *Montagues* hand is in it, who knoweth with what a diſreſpect it were to the Queen to bawke her & her miniſter here, in ſuch a caſe. Beſides in the buſineſſe it ſelf we ſhall ſuffer much, if it be ſo treated.

On fryday laſt I gaue the Pope a memoriall for his reſolution (after our ſo long patience) in your buſineſſe : vpon which he hath promiſed a ſpeedy meeting of the *Congregation* about it, & a finall determination of it. I beſeech you thank moſt humbly & hartily Sir *Iohn VVintour* in my name for his forwardneſſe to oblige me in my buſineſſe. I beg of him to continue his fauour therein, & to get her *Maieſty's* order to effect it; which I doubt not but he will haue upon his firſt mouing it to her *Maieſly.* And ſo with my humble & beſt reſpects to you, I reſt.

     Your moſt humble faithfull ſeruant.

             Kenelme Digby.

On the back : To Mr. *Fitton* 30. 7bre 1647.

Poſtcript. You can hardly imagine how troubleſone, & malicious Sir *Iohn Canſfild* is againſt all you of the *Clergy*, & any ſettlement for you; & in pa ticular beyond all meaſure againſt poore *Hyde*: whoſe fame he teareth, & proſecuteth with all violence euery where, ſharpely condemning the *Clergy* for making him *Preſident* of *Dou ay College*, an hereticall miniſter, a man of vnſound opinions in matters of faith, wrote, or ſigned ſome thing in *England* of that nature, vnfit for Gouernement, & God knoweth what not. And from him inferreth how vnfit it would be that the *Clergy* ſhould be truſted with any more important forme of *Gouernement*, then as yet th y h ue, ſince they ſtill make vſe of, & bou ſter *c. I wiſh from* out *Vnorthodox* men : c. Th s is his conſtant lai guage not only *my hart there* to Cardinal *Capponi*, & publickly in his *Anticamera* where all *was no reall* the *Engliſh* repaire; but euery where elſe, euen by way of

                                        Clamour

Clamour among *Italians* the *Pope's Ministers*, & F. *Luke*: so as he hath pressed it into the *Pope's* Eares, & giues him shrewd doubts of him: euen so much, that his Hol. asked me very odde questions of him, & shewed much vnsatisfaction. in his particular, vpon occasion of my mouing him at my last audience about his *Chanonry*. In earnest he, & Fa. *Iohn*, & the others of their party, shew themselues very factious both against you, & against the *Queen*, d. & insult most insolently of their defeating, as they beleiue, your *Chapter* businesse, though her *Maiesty* recomend it with efficacy, & I solicite it with all earnestnesse.

I pray you see what I write to Sir *Iohn VVinour* concerning Fa. *Courtney*; & silence all preiudiciall rumours in *Paris* against him.

On the back: the Postcript of my letter to Mr. Fitton 30. 7bre 1647.

[Margin: groud for this accusation; & that it were truly a Calumny. But when we consider how the Chapter Faction first boulstred out Mr. Blacklo, afterwirds Mr. Sergeant his profest disciple, & how they feare the Reputation of their Orthodox brethren such as Dr. Leybourne: we must owne this to be a great Truth.]

Another Postscript. Sir *Iohn Canffeld's*- & Fa. *Iohn's* discourse of the *English Deane & Chapter* is that the *Pope* nether can, nor ought do it, for it is against his own interest &, authority: & that therefore he refuseth it. For the *Clergy* vseth to be insolent, e. & stand vpon their owne ryghts & legs: But the *Regulars* his Missionarys depend wholy vpon his f. will; & to that accommodate themselues in euery thing. Munday 30. 7ber 1647. After I had written my Letter. Dr. *Bacon*.

d. He neuer mentioned any one particular thing done, or sayd by Sir John Canffeld, F. John against the Queen. which silence proues that to be a calumny. e. I wish there were no other proofes of this, but the words of those twa persons. f. The Regulars accommodate themselues no further to the Pope's will, then it is conformable to the will of God & the Laws of the Church. & all rules of Conscience. And so far the Secular orthodox Clergy ownes obedience to him.

most.

Most Noble Sir   Epist. 24.

I send you here a copy of a paper signed by the Prouinciaff
& by diuers *Secular Priests* as also a copy of an Oath intended to be presented by the *Catholicks* to the *Parliament*. For
my part I do not approue, nether of one, or the other:
how soeuer you may do well to shew them to his Hol. &
to the *Protectour of England*: & in case, they dislike them, you
may tell his Hol that vntill he giue the *Clergy* a superiour,

*a How
strangely is
Mr.* Fitton
*altred! the
Last year he
was so indiffe-
rent for a
Bishop, that
he seemed ra-
ther to desire
there should be
none (see
Letter* 3. &
5.) & now
Religion
*cannot stand
without one.*

b. *A fit com-
parison be-
twixt the
Obedience of
the seculare
Clergy, to the
Pope,* &

& settle Ordinary iurisdiction *a.* amorgst vs, worser things
will be done, then this is: For besides animosity, that must
needes be in the Clergy, by reason of the iniustice (as they
conceiue) of that court towards them, in denying them their
ryght, they being to suspect that that *Court* intends to introduce, & impose vpon them an *arbitrary way of Church Gouernment*, which they can no more brooke, *b.* then the *Parliament* would do *arbitrary Gouernment in the state*: & so it is not
to be wondred, if they fall into some extrauagances especially
considering that there is no superiour to restraine them, from
doing what they please. Nether will they admit of any *superiour*
without *Ordinary Iurisdiction*, & which is worse, I feare they
will not sue any more to that court for a *superiour*, if you
come downe without effecting some thing to their satiffaction ;
but seeke it elfe where as well as they can. If you please you
may giue these very words I write vnto you, to our *Protectour*,
& to whom else you please, as from me As for my self I
do not write to our *Protector*, or to any other, because (as
long as things stand thus) I will not assume vpon my self
to meddle further in that which concernes the common, then
the rest of my brethren do : & so that court must not expect
any account from vs, but take their informations from whom
they can get them, & if they be misinformed (as happily
th y may be as well as they haue been hitherto) let them
blame themselues.

                                                        Now

Now you muſt know, that this Paper, which is ſigned, *that of the* is to be diſperſed amongſt *Catholicks*, & was ſigned only for *Pirlia-* that end, that the *Cathclicks* may know how to anſwer to *ment of tht* theſe three propoſitions, which were ſent from the army to *King.* my Lord *Brudenal* in theſe very words as they lye here. There is a more ample anſwer to be drawn for the ſatiſfaction of the army, & the Parliament with a diſcourſe touching euery propoſition in particular. The beſt ieſt is, that the *Benedictins,* who were always ſuſpected to fauour the *Oath*, do now ſcruple to ſigne this paper, & (as I imagin) ſeeking to carry fauour with *Rome*, haue refuſed to do it, & yet not withſtanding their owne refuſall, they giue leaue to my Lord ⋆ *Brudenal* ⋆ *This noble* to anſwer as it is ſigned. *man before was*

As for newes &c. *ſayd to conſult* Oct. 4. Your moſt humble ſeruant *Peter Fitton* *only* Ieſuits *now none but* On the back: from Mr. Fitton 4. Octob. 1647. *Bene- d.ctins.*

✤✤✤✤✤✤✤✤✤✤✤✤✤✤✤✤✤✤✤✤✤✤✤✤✤✤✤✤✤✤✤✤✤✤✤

Oath

I A. B. Do acknowledge, teſtify, & declare in my conſcience before God, & the world, that our ſoueraign Lord K. Charles is lawfull King of this Realme, & all other his Maieſtys Realmes, dominions, & countrys. And I do promiſe, vow, & proteſt, that I will beare all faithfull, & tru allegiance to his Maieſty, his heyres, & lawfull ſucceſſors, & him & them will defend to the vttermoſt of my power againſt all Conſpiracys, & attempts whatſoeuer which ſhall be made againſt his, or their perſons, crown, & dignitys. And I will do my beſt endeauour to diſcloſe & make known to his Maieſty, his heyres, & lawfull ſucceſſors all treaſons, & traitors, or conſpiracys, which I ſhall know, or heare to be intended againſt his Maieſty, or any of them.

And

And I do abiure as falſe, & moſt erroneous both aſſaſſi-nations of Prince, & People, & that Faith is not to be ob-ſerued with all ſorts of People. And I do deteſt them both as moſt repugnant to humanity, & not to be allowed by any Religion whatſoeuer. And farther that I ſhall be moſt ready to mantain, & defend with my power, life, & fortunes all my countrys libertys, the iuſt ryghts & Libertys of Par-liaments, the ſubiects lawfull ryghts, libertys, & property, the peace & vnion of his Maieſty's three Kingdomes of Eng-land, Scotland, & Ireland, & in all iuſt, & honourable ways endeauour the Puniſhment of thoſe, that ſeeke to worke the contrary, as a dutifull & loyall ſubiect is bound to doe, & as a tru-born louer of his Country is oblidged. And that nether for hope nor fear, or other reſpects I ſhall relinquiſh this promiſe, vow, or proteſtation which I make hartily, willingly, & truly, without any equiuocation or mentall reſeruation whatſoeuer. From which as I ſhall not deſire abſolution, ſo I hold & beleiue no power on earth can abſolue me in any part.   So helpe me God.

Points.

Vpon the ground giuen in the 12.th propoſall printed Aug. the 1. 1647. by Authority from his Excellence Sir Thomas Fairfax that the penall ſtatutes inforce againſt Roman Ca-tholicks ſhall be repealed. And farther that they ſhall enioy the liberty of their Conſciences by grant from the Parliament, it may be enacted that it ſhall not be lawfull for any per-ſon, or perſons being ſubiects to the Crown of England to profeſſe, or acknowledge for truth, or perſwade others to beleiue the enſuing propoſitions.

1 That the Pope, or Church hath power to abſolue any perſon, or perſons whatſoeuer from his, or their obedience to the ciuil gouernment eſtabliſht in this nation.

2 That it is lawfull in it ſelf, or by the Pope's Diſpenſa-tion, to break ether word, or oath with any Heretick.

3 That

3 That it is lawfull by the Pope's, or Church's command, or difpenfation to kill, deftroy, or otherwife iniure, or offend any perfon, or perfons whatfoeuer, becaufe he, or they are accufed, condemned, cenfured, or excommunicated for errour, fchifm or herefy.

The premiffes confidered, we vnder written fet our hands, that euery one of thefe three propofitions may be lawfully anfwered vnto in the negatiue.

On the back: The Oath Points.

❀❁❀❁❀❁❀❁❀❁❀❁❀❁❀❁❀❁❀❁❀❁❀❁❀❁❀❁❀❁❀❁❀

Sir Ken. D. to Mr. Fitton

Rome 7. 8ber 1647.

Mofthonoured Sir   *Epift.* 26.

You would be extreamely to blame, beyond all capacity of Pardon, *a.* if for any weak refpects to this court (which yeild you none) you fhould forbear making vfe of that happy coniuncture of affayres to procure your own aduantages, which God *b.* hath opened you a dore vnto. The Pope, & his minifters apprehend you will not; but I conceiue you will do, what wife men in your cafes would do. And therefore the *Pope* is in mind to fend a Perfon to refide about the *Queen* who vnder pretence of her feruice may get countenance from her *Maiefty*, befides the authority he fhall bring with him from his mafter to keep you in aw, & embroyle your *c.* affayres. The perfon he hath pitched vpon is fignr. *Ferrante Capponi*, whom I conceiue you know well. But this, as from me, you muft keep exceeding fecret. For as yet if it be vented, whiles only three perfons in this court befides my felf

a. Here is a new fin againft the Holy Ghoft, not to be forgiuen in this world, nor the next, to retain any confideration for the Sea Apoftolick.

self do know it, there myght ensue great harme to who is my confident. Knowing his end, & his *instructions*, I do what I can by all dextrous meanes to suspend his going, that you may haue time to do your businesse first with the *Army* & *Parliament*. I must with all giue you account of another thing, but in as great confidence as I can say any thing, & I con-iure you let no body but Mr. *Holden* know any thing of this no more then of the former secret. It is that le P. *Giles Chaissy* at *London* is the man that mouldeth, & manageth all the *Ca-tholicks* businesse with the state there & sendeth a weekely account hither, & receiueth weekely *Instructions* from hence. You looke vpon my Lord *Brudenall*, & Mr. *Montagu*; but it is *Monsieur de S. Giles* (or le *Pere Giles*) that is the soule, who guides those Organs. And he disposeth all he can to haue a strict dependance of the see of *Rome*, expecting speedily from hence a *Bishoprick* in reward *d.* of his Labours. Beleiue this is a certain truth, for I know it. Only make vse of the aduice in the gouerning your own affaires, & in speedy putting them to an issue.

I hear nothing from Sir *Iohn Wintour*, or any of our court this weeke. I slacken no endeaueurs for your seruice here. So humbly thanking you for yours of the 13. past I rest

Your most humble faithfull seruant

Kenelme Digby.

On the back: To Mr. *Fitton* 7. *octob.* 1647.

I most

❀❀ ❀❀❀❀❀❀❀❀❀❀❀❀❀❀❀❀❀❀❀❀❀❀❀❀❀❀❀

Rome 7. of 8ber 1647.

Sir   *Epiſt. 27.*

I moſt humbly thank you for yours of the 13. paſt, & re-joyce to ſee that our vnhappy country is not yet ſo forlorne, but that there is one man of wit, & courage, ſeaſoned with piety *a*. who hath care of it. Your *printed paper*, & *written inſtructions were all dictated by the Holy Ghoſt. b.* But act: let not all end in deſigning, & diſcourſing. By any meanes print a-gain your former Dialogue. Cloſe with the *Independants. c.* Make them ſee their intereſt to ſtrengthen themſelues, by vnion with *Catholick party,* which may adhere to them, when after the *Parliament* & *Army* diſſolved, the *Presbiterians* will grow too hard for them ſingle. And doe all you can juſtly to compaſſe fitt conditions & aduantages for vs, without mingling this wicked & intereſſed court *d.* in our treaties: for I dare aſſure you, they will cooperate nothing to your good, but dependently of their own ends; & will endeauour to keep vs always like *VVardes* in a very ſeruile pupillage. I wiſh with all my hart I were now in *England:* for in this great worke I would gladly employ not only my paines, but my fortune, & my life. And vnder your direction I ſhould hope, that the *intereſt* I haue with the *now ruling e.* perſons, & ſuch little knowledge as I haue in affaires of the world, & particularly of this na-ture myght produce ſome good worth leauing a deſert for at leaſt for ſo long a time, as would take vp that treaty. And I ſhould not care whom I diſpleaſed, *f.* ſo I compaſſed the Catholicks juſt endes. But God knoweth beſt who, & what is beſt for euery perſon & buſineſſe. And to his prouidence I quietly ſubmit all.

I pray you vſe your vtmoſt endeaueur to get P. *Barbanſon's Anatomia Anima,* by meanes of your book ſellers or freinds

from

a. VVe ſee the opinion Sir Kenelme Digby *had of* Dr. Hol-den, *for pen-ning as he did* thoſe In-ſtructions. *How iuſtly he deſerued this elogium let others gueſſe. That he ſhewed* Courage, I *grant,* & *alſo ſome wit; but* I deny *that there is any footſtep of* Pi-ety *in it.*

b. Yet I beleiue nether the one nor the other will euer be admitted into the Canon of H. Scripture.

from *Flanders*, or *Cullen*; for I heare it is the beſt, the ſolideſt, the ſubtileſt, & the hygheſt book that hath euer been written in that kind.

I ſhall haue extreame difficulty, (if not impoſſibility) *g.* to get the licence you aſke for *Dna Lucia de Rochefoucault*. Therefore I will expect your peremptory command to do all I can *per fas & nefas* to purchaſe it, before I embarke my ſelf with engaging all my ſtrength for it. That is, conſider of your ſelf whither it be of that importance or no, to be worth the labour.

c. A good aduice for one who was actually employed by the Queen!

Mr. *VVhite's* book wil certainly be cenſured if I do not a miracle to preſerue it. That buſineſſe was very ill caſt, that the fagot of bookes was not directed to me; but looſely turned into the *Dogana* in a bookeſellers bale. It will be neceſſary that he dilate, & confirme the doctrine there of *Originall ſinn*, & of *non exiſtence of Accidents without ſubiects*. I pray God preſerue *Mrs Girbiers* from all misfortunes; but I feare the worſt. Indeed the Abbot hath bin much too blame.

d. He muſt always haue a fling at Rome: ſo dutifull a ſon is he of the Roman Church.

I am Entirely yours Kenelme Digby.

On the back: to Dr. Holden 7. 8ber 1647.

e. He flattred himſelf extreamely with the opinion of his intereſt: which how inconſiderable it was we ſhall ſee Letter 46. f. This zeale, & contempt of Humane reſpects, would be commendable, if directed by Prudence, & ſubiect to tru Charity to promote the common good, but being reſtrained to the illegall deſignes of one part, (which he calls Juſt ends) it is factious, & blame worthy. g. It is ſtrang, that he who ſo lately boaſted of his hauing the whole Court of Rome at his beck, who could baniſh, or retain men as he pleaſed, ſhould now think it impoſible to procure ſo ſlyght a buſineſſe, as this, viz, Leaue for a Lady to enter into a monaſtery of women!

moſt

Rome 14 Octob. 1647.

Most Hond Sir   *Epist.* 28.

I humbly thank you for yours of the 20. past. My cheife businesse *a.* is now, & hath bin this good while to presse for *a resolution,* on or off, of your *Chapter* businesse as conceiuing I may hue speedily order to depart from hence & that it is as good as lost, if I leaue it then depending. But all my industry & Art hath not as yet bin able to obtain other answer, but that his Holinesse is resolued forthwith to giue all satisfaction to the *English Clergy,* as that which he *b.* esteemeth in a hygh mesure for their Piety, their constancy in their great prosecutions, & their Eminent Learning. But he doth nothing in the businesse, nor will enter into the particulars of it: but accordeth me all in generall, & referreth me to the *Congregation* to draw vp, & ajust particulars: And this *Benedetta Congregatione* I can neuer get to meet. *c.* Card. *Capponi* doth his vtmost to procure their assembling, assuring me, that they nether can, nor dare deny what you aske. But withall his *Emin.* beleiueth they will seeke what they can to shift it off for the present, & lay hold of all pretences for delay. Yet he is confident he shall driue them from all their Euasions, though he stand single for you, & all the rest be joyned against you. The *Pope* since the creation of the Card. Of *Aix* laugheth *d.* at all that hath been insinuated vnto him, of the English Clergy procuring Bishops from the French, which at first did move him vehemently. But now he maketh account he hath *France* at his beck: he sayeth himself he hath that Kingdom in *suo pugno*: & that now Card. *Mazarin* for his Brothers promotion will obsequiously, & implicitly obey whatsoeuer his Ho: shall wish him to do. So that he speaketh confidently, that if the Arch Bishop

a. It's strange that the cheife businesse of a publick minister of so great a Princesse, who had so many then on her hands should be to solicit private concern of one part of the Kingdom. Had he no other? or did not regard any other? Deberet fortè esse Persecutió.

b. The bulk of the English secular Clergy, deserues this,

of

& greater commendations: & it is Lamentable those of vertu & learning should be trampled on by the black-loistical & factious part.

of *Rouen* fhould but entertain any fute of our *Clergy's* to fuch purpofe, as hath bin whifpered here to him, the Card. *Mazarin* vpon the leaft word of his Ho: would fend him prifoner to the *Baftile*, or any other fhould dare to coun-tenance the *English Clergy* to ftand vppon their owne legges. Truly I conceiue vppon rhe whole matter that bufineffe is now vpon fuch termes, as if you fhould not haue faire Sa-tiffaction before I depart from hence, it importeth both the *Queen* & you, & all the *Catholickes* of *England*, to proceede in fuch a courfe as reafon & Juftice fhall warrant you in: & that without it, after fuch intimations (not to fay threates) of what you will do, you muft euer henceforward expect e to be very ill vfed, & troden vpon. And fo I pray God to

c. So inconfi-derable had he made himfelf, by embraceing blindly all the concernes of

fend you all happineffe, refting

Your moft humble & affectionate feruant

Kenelme Digby.

On the back .To Mr· Fitton 14. Octob. 1647.

that Faction. *d. Here is* non caufa pro caufa. *From the beginning his Holineffe little regarded thofe threates of* Bifhops *from France. He knew too well their zeale for the vnity of the* Church, *to feare that. Other things olleadged by Sir Ke-nelme moued him more viz., the credit of the* Party *with the* Independants. *But find-ing that to be imaginary, he looked on all thofe threats as words. & no more. e. Here he exhortes the* Secular Clergy *to lay afide all thoughts of redreffe from* Rome: *& charges the bad fucceffe of his negociation not on his ill management of it, nor on the threates with which it was accompanyed, & which to fuperiours are always moft odious; but on the* Little *regard that court had for the* Sec. Clergy. *Which either is falfe, or if tru, it was caufed by the faults of the preuailing factious Party in it, & would be changed, affoone as the offending caufe was remoued. It was therfore his Duty to haue reprefented to thofe men the tru ground of that alienation (if there were any) of his* Holineffe *& his* Minifters *from the* English Sec. Clergy. *But this he would not do, the Doctrine of his* Oracle, *Mr.* Blacklo, *being concerned in it. And his own : For the Diuinity of this Man is drawn, not out of* Scrip-ture, Tradition, Councils, Decretals, Fathers, *the vfual & only fountaines, of all* Diuinity; *but as he fays himfelf, out of the* DIGBEAN PHILOSOPHY.

most

Most Noble Sir   *Epiſt.* 29.

I Hope that this Letter will find you yet in Rome, which if
it do I would entreat you in caſe that our buſineſſe is not
come to a concluſion, that you would procure at Leaſtways
a Letter from our Protectour to this purpoſe, that we may
proceed on with our deanes & chapter, *a.* as we haue don   *a. The deſpe-*
hitherto vntill ſuch time as it ſhall be otherwiſe ordained by   *rate condition,*
his Hol:& that in the mean time the Dean may enjoy the   *which this*
facultyes formerly granted to the Arch prieſt. This is a thing   *Letter repre-*
which the Protectour may do without recurring to the con-   *ſents the*
greg. by ſpeaking a word only to his Hol. & by receiuing   chapters
order from him *viva vocis oraculc:* or if you your ſelf could pro-   Confirma -
poſe it to his Hol. I doubt not but he will tell you we may;   tion *to be in*
which will ſuffice vs without propoſing to the congr. who in all   *proves my*
likelihood will deny this as they haue done all the reſt. You   *cniecture.*
may ſhew his Hol. or our Protectour the neceſſity of it,   *tha the tru*
becauſe otherwiſe we ſhall be left for the interim without all   *cauſe of the*
Gouernment *b.* which muſt needes breed great harme and   *miſcarriage*
confuſion, & there can be no prejudice to the Pope to grant   *of that affaire*
this, it being only for an interim.   *uas the*
    I ſend you here the copy *c.* of a Paper deliuered to Crom-   *threats they*
well & Ireton ſigned by 5. or 6. Lord's & 50. other gen-   *vſed hoping*
tlemen of quality, together with this paper they deliuered a   *thereby to*
petition, which Cromwell & Ireton promiſt to deliuer to the   *quicken the*
Parliament, in du time, as a thing avowed & approved by the   *diſpa·ch,*
whole army.   *whicl fll*
    I ſuppoſe you haue ſeen a printed paper ſet forth by   *out quite*
Dr. *Holden*, which is much cryed out againſt in *England*, &   *otherwiſe: for*
as I hear intended to: be diſowned by the Catholicks. *d.*   *from th at time*
Mr. *Montagu* in particular I hear is extreamely offended at it   *their hopes*
although the things that exception is taken againſt I ſuppoſe   *uiſibly dimi-*
e. the greateſt oppoſition proceedeth from Regulars out of   *niſht, till at*
                        animoſity

last they quite vanisht. And those, whome lately nothing could satisfy, but an absolute acknowledgment of their vncanonical Chapter, & Many Bishops, would now be satisfyed with an ordinarily Letter from the

animosity, are 1. those words: *except perhaps in the Pope his Dominions.* 2. Those words: *Some rigorous proceedings of the court of Rome, & seuerall seditious combinations,* &c. 3. Those words: *if you find amongst your Petitioners any dregs of those pragmaticall plotters &c* 4. those words: *(which being a pure gift of God ought not to be forced, or violented vpon any)* Lastly the King is offended that he Joines him, & the *Parliament* together. I thought good to aduertise you of this, because it may be, you will hear more noyse of it there. &c.

Your most humble seruant   Peter Fitton.

Being ready to seale vp my Letter, I receiued your of sept. 23. And assure you selfe that if an *Oath* be necessary, we shall do (as you aduise) that which is just, let that Court think of it what they please.

On the back: from Mr. Fitton 18. octob. 1647.

substitute of the Protectour, (*Cardinal* Barbarin *the* Protectour *being absent*) *with a prouisional allowance of the* Chapter, *till the* Pope *provide another Gouernour. I wish by this lamentable experience they would learn, that sturdy Beggars are odious, & that Petitioners ought not to threaten with a Cudgal, as not demanding; but commanding. b.* Subiumo: *but there was no such Letter granted: ergo the* Secular Clergy *is left without all Gouernment. I wish those would consider this, who stand so stifly for the Authority of the pretended Chapter, & call all those seditious men, who doubt of its authority: altho there is none, who vnderstands it, but must doubt of it. c. The Paper follows after this Letter. The Petition I could neuer find. d. No lesse could be expected from any wise, & moderate men, then a dislike in Generall of such an attempt of a priuate pragmatical man in a business of general concern, in which he ought not to haue medled without the order, or at least advice of the rest. I wonder Mr.* Holden *did not in a huffe go ouer into* England, *to the* Army, *& either vnite to his sentiments the foolish* Catholicks, *or hang them. As he very meekely sayd in his Letter of the* 6. *of September. Vide Lit* 15.

e. Vppon what is this supposition grounded of Regulars *opposing this Act, but that all things which displease these men must proceed from* Regulars, *& be charged* *on them ? Cannot the King be displeased to see himself ranked with the Parliament, that is a Soueraign with his subiects , vnlesse he haue a Benedictin , or a Dominican at his elbow , to moue him to it ? Cannot the Catholick Nobility be offended to see the Pope & his Ministers accused & censured & their Catholick Ancestors condemned , vnlesse a Franciscan , or Jesuit stir them to it ? Hath nether King , nor Lord nor Gentleman , nor Commoner any sense of wrongs don to them, the Church , or state , but what they receiue from Regulars ? But it seemes Regulars must be charged with all odious , & displeasing matters , ryght or wrong , it matters not. No wonder Protestants should charge all mischeifs on Papists. They deal with them , as the secular Clergy do with Regulars.*

✦✦✦✦✦✦✦✦✦✦✦✦✦✦✦✦✦✦✦✦✦✦✦✦✦✦✦✦✦✦✦✦✦✦

This Act vvas deliuered to the Army by 5. or 6. Lords & some 50. other persons of quality.

The Roman Catholicks of this Kingdome taking into con-sideration the 12. proposall in the declaration of his Excel. Sir Thomas Fairfax lately published this present year 1647. And how prejudiciall & destructiue it myght be to them, at this time tacitely to permit an opinion (by some conceiued) of an inconsistency in their Religion with the civil Gouern-ment of this Kingdom, by reason of some doctrines and positions scandalously layd vpon them , which myght thereby draw on persons, that cannot conforme themselues to the Religion here established, an incapacity to receiue, & be partakers of a Generall benefit intended for the ease of ten-der consciences : haue thorght it conuenient to endeauour the just vindication of their integrityes therein : & to remoue the scandall out of all the minds, & opinions of moderate, & charitable persons, do declare the negative to those pro-positions following.

1. That the Pope, or Church hath power to absolue any
person

perſons, or perſons whatſoeuer from his or their Obedience to the civill government eſtabliſhed in this Nation.

2 That it is lawfull by the Pope's or Church's command or diſpenſation, to kill, deſtroy, or other wiſe injure any perſon or perſons, vnder his Majeſty's dominions, becauſe he or they are accuſed, or condemned, cenſured, or excommunicated for any errour ſchiſme or hereſy.

3 That it is lawfull in it ſelf, or by the Popes diſpenſation to break ether word, or oath with any perſons aboue-ſayd, vnder pretence of their being hereticks.

And in further teſtimony that we diſavow the ſayd precedent propoſitions, as being no part of our faith, ✶ or euer taught vs by our Paſtors, we haue here-ratifyed the ſame vnder our hands.

On the back: The Act ſigned by the Catholick Lords, &others.

✶ *I do not beleiue, that euer any Catholick Doctor thought, writ, or taught that thoſe Poſitions, or any of them were to be held for articles of the Catholick Faith, deliuered by Chriſt to his Apoſtles, & by them, & their ſucceſſours handed thorough all ages down to vs.*

❀✦❀✦❀✦❀✦❀✦❀✦❀✦❀✦❀✦❀✦❀✦❀✦❀✦❀✦❀✦❀✦❀✦❀✦❀✦

Agentis Cleri Supplicatio ad ſumum Pontificem Ex Italico tranſlata.

Beatiſſime Pater.

Agens Cleri Anglicani humilitèr exponit Sanctitati veſtræ, quod in Angliâ ob defectum Epiſcopi, vel alterius, qui rebus Eccleſiaſticis præſit, aut pro ſuperiore agnoſcatur, omnes functiones ſacræ obeuntur confuſè & inordinatè adminiſtráturque Sacramenta ſine facultate, & iuriſdictione, cum nemo
certus

certus fit in regno, à quo obtineri queat, nec recurri poſſit ad Superiores tranſmarinos ob multas & notas difficultates. Ex quo oriuntur indies præter innumera alia inconvenientia & ſcandala, nullitates & invaliditates Matrimoniorum, Con-feſſionum, &c. cui vt in poſterum occurratur, ſupplicatur humiliter Sanctitati veſtræ, vt dignetur benignè deputare v-num vel duos Sacerdotes in regno qui proviſionaliter conce-dant & communicent aliis facultates neceſſarias ad legitimam adminiſtrationem Sacramentorum, donec Sanctitas veſtra vlte-rius quid reſoluat circa Conceſſionem Epiſcopi, vel alius Su-perioris legitimi dictorum fidelium, & Cleri.   Quod &c. Quam Deus &c.

Note: when this Petition was preſented to his Holineſſe I cannot tell: certainly it was ſince the return of Sir K. D. re infectà. VVe ſee here an acknowledgment like that of Mr. Fitton *in his foregoing Letter, of the nullity of the* Chapter

❀❀➢❀❀ ➣❀❀➣❀❀➢❀❀➢❀❀➢❀❀❀❀❀➣❀❀➢❀❀➢❀❀❀❀❀❀➣❀❀

Sir Kenel. D. to Dr. Holden.

Rome 21. 8ber 1647.

Sir

EpiſT. 32.

After my late Letter from hence (in which I haue giuen account of the ſtate of affayres here) & vpon your know-ledge how I haue long expected my reuocation (& there-fore it were vnſeaſonable to engage my ſelf in new buſineſſe) you will expect by this poſt little more from me, then to acknowledge the receipt of yours of the 26. paſt. Yet I preſs for an iſſue & concluſion of the *Clergys* buſineſſe: So that I hope to obtain ſpeedily a meeting of the *Congregation*, & a reſolution. Yet I muſt tell you, that if I preuaile to haue
the

the *Cardinalls* meet it is an act of meer importunity & violence : for nothing can be more against their mindes. They dare not giue vs a flat deniall *a.* of that Church Gouerment which *Christ* setled in his whole *Church.* And on the other side they are so imbued with a beleife of the *secular Clergys* retractory, & turbulent spirit, *b.* that if it be possible, they will euade coming to a conclusion. Sir *Iohn Canffeld* hath been much to blame . & very injurious to you. He cryeth a main of your whole œconomy of *Gouernment*, & against the persons of your Gouernours. Mr. *Gage* & Mr. *Hyde* are two principall markes, he aimeth at. He hath much blasted the later to hinder his obtaining a *Canonry.* And it is reported here from his mouth, that there are not above 8. *Alumni* at *Deway*, & that the allowance which the *Pope* maketh vnto that Colledge is conuerted to far different vses, then is intended by the giuer. Indeed he is a very froward spirit, which maketh me be very sorry, that he hath gotten an employment, & Letter, & mony from this court into *Ireland* : for he professeth he will set all on fire. If he had not bin recommended hither by the *Queenes* Letters he would not haue had the credit to do these mischeifes : But for her *Majestys* sake he had respect, & credence here especially when he made vse of it according to the sentiments of the People. The *French Ambaffader* nether can, nor will do any thing for him. Much lesse can I, who would most hartily, nor any man else. This *Pope* will do no *graces* : who of all men liuing hath least reason to put him self vpon the rigor of *Gods justice*, if it be tru that is sayd of him. I haue nothing to trouble Mr. *Fitton* with particularly this weeke : & I make account that what I say to one of you I say to both. I humbly thank him for his of the same date with yours, & I pray you tell him, you of the Clergy are out of the way, *c.* as long, as you solicit to haue any good from hence. Abandon not your selues. And when Justice is denyed or delayed you here, seeke it elsewhere. And remember, that they are only duped here , who haue a mind to be
so

a. The Pope hath great reason to stand in awe of halfe a dozen Blacloists.

b. I think this is tru.

c. The Secular Clergy will be well guided, if it

so. It istru his Hol. is grown confident, & bold, & begineth to speak big language & expreffeth a great contempt of vs, & what we can do, d. fince he hath oblidged Card. *Mazarin* by promoting his Brother: beleiueth himfelf now able to difpofe of all *France* at his Beck: & that an *Arch Bishop* of *Rouen*, or euen the whole *Clergy* of *France* & *Colledge* of the *Sorbone* will be made fay any thing he defires vpon a bare Letter to Card. *Mazarin*. But I hope better of the Cardinals Prudence & Piety, and of your Church men's Judgment, & courage, then that we fhall be abandoned to neglect, & fold into the fervitude of our enemys, at the price of a red Cap.

Juft as I was writing what is aboue, F. Prefident *Iohn VVilfrid* e. came to fee me, with great proteftations of duty, & affection to the *Queen*, & of refpect to me. Vnto which I replyed that I had no ill talent to his perfon euen when I Laboured with my vtmoft induftry that no offices or endeauours of his myght prejudice ether her Majeftys feruice, or the Clergys intereft.

I intend ere long to return him his vifit. Vpon which I hope Sir *Iohn VVintour* will be well fatisfyed of me: who hath written to me feuerall times with much earneftneffe, to receiue, & vfe him fairly, if he fhould come with refpect vnto me. It is now time for me to leaue you to your better thoughts. Only I muft entreat you to get for me *le fatum de Monfieur le Marechal de la Motte Houdancourt contre Monfieur le le Procureur General du Roy au Parlement de Grenoble.* And fo remembring my humbly feruice to Mr. *Fitton*, & hoping ere long to fee you (therefore after your receiuing this write no more to me) I take my Leaue, & reft

Yours entirely Kenelme Digby.

On the back. to Dr. Holden 21. 8ber 1647.

followes Sir K. D. directions.

d. I haue elfewhere giuen the tru reafon of this chang in the Pope s Language, viz, the vain menace vfed in the name of the English Clergy.

e. This R. Father was to be banisht with F. Courtney, had Sir K. preuailed: but failing he faignes a fubmiffion, to faue his own credit.

moft

❀❀❀❀❀❀❀❀❀❀❀❀❀❀❀❀❀❀❀❀❀❀❀❀❀❀❀❀❀❀

Rome 28. 8ber 1647.

Mosthonoured Sir   *Epist.* 33.

I haue yours of the 4. current, which I humbly thank you for: I cannot difcern what it is you miflike in the Oath, & Propofitions, vnleffe it be that you feare they are not home enough to fatiffy the *Independents*: for I fee no caufe for *Catholicks* to make any fcruple at them. We do weakely to hazard our vndoing for this court, that hath no Piety, nor Charity for vs, nor confidereth vs beyond their private fordid intereft. Without all doubt thefe Propofitions, as they are vniverfall ones, & not limited to particular cafes, ought to be fubfcribed by euery good fubiect. Fa. *Iohn* (who now is moft kind to me, & vifiteth me dayly) is of that mind. And you fhall hereafter fee the *Benedictins* as forward, as any of the pack. Father Rector here of the *Iefuits* hath giuen in a copy of all, & afketh directions how to fteere in this fea, & there is a congregation of 16. Diuines (but hitherto very private) to fit vppon it, & give their opinions to the *Pope*. It is a great fault to aske leave, when we need not, & where we are fure to haue the queftion pared, & Limited to their owne felf intereft. Though I haue ferved you little here, I am not out of hope of being confiderably vfefull to you in England, *a.* as things ftand. Card. *Capponi* hath giuen me his Letter to you, & to your canons *b.* in England. They are the fame, (as he telleth me) that he fhewed me 9. or 10. months agoe, & differed them till now, vppon expectation euery weeke to haue your *Chapter* bufineffe done to your mind. But he hath now loft all credit at court, I may fafely fay, for yours, *c.* & the Queene's fake, in both whofe interefts he hath appeared boldly, & fpoken lowdly. Yet I fend you not the Letters till next weeke, conceiuing it poffible there may be fome fuddain change here in refolutions con-

a. He flatters himfelf with expectations of great fucceffe in England: where as hard fate expected him, & much harder as we

concerniug

Concerning vs. I am withall fincerity
shall fee his

Your moft humble & faithfull fervant. letter 17.

K. Digby. 1650.

On the back. To Mr. Fitton 28. octob. 1647

b. Thefe are not fuch Let-ters as Mr. Fitton *demanded Letter* 28. *c. That that good* Cardinal *left his credit, favouring* Blackloifts, *I eafily beleive, but that his zeale for the* Queen's *fervice fhould prejudice him, is improbable.*

❖❖❖❖❖❖❖❖❖❖❖❖❖❖❖·❖❖❖❖❖❖❖❖❖❖❖❖❖❖❖❖❖

Mr. Thomas VVhite to Sir K. D.

Moft honoured Sir   *Epift. 34.*

Thefe are to humbly thank you, for yours of the 14. of
octob. & more for the paines I haue vnluckily put you vnto
by fending you my bookes. The packet whereof had no o-
ther addreffe from me, but vnto your felf: howfoeuer for
its littleneffe I fuppofe it was put into a greater to Mr. Trichet.
I doe not care what they doe with the bookes, & fhould
not bee much forry *a.* if they cenfured them. Onely it troub-
leth me to haue put you into an harfh bufineffe. If the refufall of the Chapter can Demanife Mr. Fitton, *b.* it will doe
nore good, then the Confirmation would haue done. Mr.
Hyde is extremely bound vnto you, & I vpon new refpects
for the good will you fhew him. But I fhould be forry you
fhould ftay an hour in Rone to the prejudice of your health,
for any of our occafions. I feare you will be troubled with
the council of Conftance. For the reft I feare not what will be
cited out of F. F. & CC. Thofe who write againft the motion of the Earth, or indifferently, generally conclude that
fcripture *c.* convinceth nothing which neverthel--ffe is the

a. How little doth he regard the Roman Cenfures!

b. Doe thefe words fpeake an vnderva-luing of the approbation of the Chap-ter, or a

ground

desire of Mr. Fitton's abandoning Rome? *Anger spocke them, that their affaires in* Rome *should be disappointed.*

ground of their decree, as *Marinus, Gaßandus,* & I think *Bromondus.* I am told that a *Iesuite* in this town hath a Load-stone soe strong, that if a man keep the Iron from it with all his force, it will draw man & all to it self. I shall see what news I can get from Mr. *Chantond* againft your coming. There is another in town hath promised me the same, & sayeth he hath two other secretts, the one to tinct *Luna* to yeild 30 for one: the other to draw a crown of gold out of an ounce of *Luna..* He is poore, but not needy, & hath a modest caraige. By the time you com I shall see whither he be worth your acqvaintance. Mr. *Skinner* prefenteth his humble respects vnto you, & desireth you would permit one of your Laquais to carry this enclosed to Mr. *Hart.* God send you well & soon back.

t. Mr. Blacklo foisted sayd Dr. Leybourne *into* Rusworth's *dialogues a more general Errour, viz, that*

Your most humble & affectionate freind & servant

Thomas White.

Lyons octob. 31.

It is long since I am acquainted with *sendovigius* vpon Dr. *Mores* recommendation. But I fear I shall vnderstand little in him.

On the back. From Mr. White 31. 8ber. 1647.

Scripture was no Fitter to convince any thing, then a Beetle to cut, or a straw to knock with. *VVhich* R. Smith *late* Bishop *of* Calcedon *sayd was a* Blasphemy: *& expreßely contrary to the Apostle:* Omnis Scriptura divinitus inspirata vtilis est ad redarguendum.

✦✧✦✧✦✧✦✧✦✧✦✧✦✧✦✧✦✧✦✧✦✧✦✧✦✧✦✧✦✧

Sir Ken. D. to Dr. Holden.

Rome 18. nou. 1647.

Sir

Epist. 35.

This is in answer of yours of the 25. of 8ber. your commands in which of making what hast I can to you, shall be obayed

obeyed by me. And if vnder your wing & directions, I may doe any good there, I resigne my self in your handes: do with me as you pleafe, & in all things I will steere by the compaffe you shall affign me. *a.* I cannot fufficiently admire at the folly *b.* of our *Enlish Catholicks*, who will depend so contemptibly vpon this wicked intereffed court, that neither careth for them, nor efteemeth them. But I am perswaded this Pope will do great good in this particular if *God* permit him (for the advantage of his Church) to live a little longer: for his infamous covetousneffe, & neglect of Gods fervice is fo groff that every body beginneth to be weaned from this Childifhneffe, & to deteft thofe *Mamens* of *iniquity*, & to do their bufineffe *c.* qvietly by themfelves. I had long difcourfe yefterday with the Pope about Mr. Whites book, & gave him a memoriall concerning it : I know not yet what will be the effect. The *Magifter Sacri Palatij* is a fcrupulous drye *Pedant d.* & is now bufie cenfuring a Iefuits book of Palermo, that holdeth a like opinion to Mr. Whites concerning the appearing accidents in the Bleffed Sacrament. I gave Sir *Iohn Canffield* more refpect, then belonged to him. But fuch intollerable pride, & felf conceite *e.* as he hath is never fatisfyed. My former letters will haue told you, I can do nothing for Monfueir *le Gras.* And this will affure I am
Entirely yours   Kenelme Digby.

On the back: to Dr. Holden 18. nou 1647.

his *Cenfures very liberally: & no wonder, for none can pleafe him, but the* All-knowing Blacklo. *Thefe Cenfures fpeak Sir* Kenelme's *Humility.*

most

a. He will then fayle in danger of shipu rack.

b. Another exhortation to break from Rome, that is, to a fchifme.

c. To embrace which (fchifme) he alleadges the example of others, which nobody heard of befides himfelf vnleße it were from him.

d. He beftows

✪꙰꙰꙰꙰꙰꙰꙰꙰꙰꙰꙰꙰꙰꙰꙰꙰꙰꙰꙰꙰꙰꙰꙰꙰꙰꙰꙰꙰

Rome 18. nou. 1647.

Most honoured Sir   *Epist.* 36.

I am indebt to you for Letters of the 9. & 30. of Aug. & of the 20. 7ber. My flow payment hath proceeded from my weekely hopes of obtaining the promise of a *Chanonry* for you, (notwithstanding all your enemys opposition) that so my Letter myght be the more welcom to you, then whilst it should carry with it barren expressions of my respects. And this my neere hopes fluttering still before me hath drawne me into this great arrear: for which I humbly aske your pardon. Yesterday I got the Popes promise for you of the chanonry vacant by the death of Monsieur *del Clef,* who dyed 14. 8ber last. I had notice of it by Mr. *Fittons* Letter just as I was going to my audience: & so I hastily scribled a note my self, whereby to fix the Popes promise so as to ground vpon it the speeding of the bulles, without danger of his saying afterwards he forgott it & had there-vpon given it a nother. I have also sent for Signior *Zatti* to follow it at the *Datary;* & I haue spoken to Dr. *Bacon* to do the like : & haue already likewise recommended it to Card. *Capponi,* to lend his hand to it, if there should arise some difficulty : which truly I doubt nor, but in such cases, in these times one cannot be to sure.

a. Of these we neuer saw any signe, but in this Letter.

    The french Ambassadour hath spoken efficaciously *a.* to the Pope to confirm your *Deane & chapter;* & further to give vs *Bishops* : so farre he is from what is told you. I had large discourse yesterday with his Hol. here abouts: & he alloweth positively all I aske ; only he is advised to delay time before he settle things, till he see what plye the affayres of those in *England* will take. Yett he assured me yesterday he would before my departure take some order to giue content to the *Clergy.* He is of a nature easily diverted from doing any thing

thing, in any kind. But he is so inefficacious *b.* in all things *b. Of late there*
of action (excepting accumulating mony) that such thoughts *hath beene no*
vsually passe not beyond impotent wishes. There was neuer *Pope, to*
any the least declaration of the *Congregation* against the *Deane whom this*
& chapter. They dare *c.* not discountenance it, much lesse *could be lesse*
deny it. But all the Cardinalls of it excepting *C. Cipponi,* & *reproached,*
Monsigneur *Albizi* , are so divoted to the interests of *as appeared by*
some *Regulars* (& for some other regard) that they seek to *many in-*
coole the heate which my pressures putt in the businesse, *stances.*
by gaining time, especially till I should be gone : & then
they hope they shall rest a while vnmolested : for I spare *c. This is sayd*
them not. But rest you confident that happen the worst that *to encourage*
may be, they neither can nor will, nor *d,* dare declare anie *the Party in*
the least blemish against you, whatsoever they may whisper, *their huffing*
& murmur amongst themselues. I must do the *Pope,* & our *way, which*
Cardinall *Protectour* this ryght, vpon this occasion, that truly *hath ruined*
the former is well affected towards you, & your businesse : *their credit in*
& the latter is passionate, & earnest for you. I may chance *Rome.*
go now away from hence with both giving & receiving some
disgust : for I have dealed very freely & planely with the *Pope,* *d. They both*
as Mr. *Fitton* can inform you more particularly : And it is *dare & haue*
not new that truth frankly spoken should beget Enemyes. *declared a-*
I reckon them not, as long as that raiseth them, be they never *gainst them,*
so powerfull. He that neither hopeth, nor feareth any thing *when they*
in this world, hath a great advantage. And as little I am *condemned all*
moved at the various discourses, which passe of me, to my *Blackloe's*
prejudice . But much to see your great kindnesse & frend- *bookes, whose*
linesse to me which I beseech you continu, & beleive me to be *Protection*
worthy Sir   Your most humble & affectionate servant *they had vn-*
           Kenelme Digby.   *dertaken.*

On the back : to Dr. *Hyde* President of Doway 18. nou.
1647.

❖❖❖❖❖❖❖❖❖❖❖❖❖❖❖❖❖❖❖❖❖❖❖❖❖❖❖❖❖❖

Rome 25. nou. 1647.

Most honoured Sir   *Epist.* 37.

I haue yours of the 4. cur. The thought of sending Signeur *Ferrante* was changed vnto Monsieur de *Ceritantes,* who (to tell you tru) I thought by no meanes so fit (all things considered, for he is Card. *Spada's* creature, & Monsigneur *Albezi's* botome freind) as the other: therefore I represented to him the rockes he myght run vpon, & steered him as dextrously, as I could to take hold of greater hopes, that dawne to him by accompanying the Duke *Gvise,* to *Naples:* where he now is the Minister for the Crowne of France: for the D. of *Gvise,* goeth vpon his owne score with the *Napolitanes* without any dependance of *France,* but their leave to advantage himself what he can, expecting only assistance, & countenance from *France,* for their owne interests in infeebling the Monorky of *Spaine.* So that now the treaty is come back vpon Signeur *Ferrante* against, whose great rubb is matter of mony, for he will not spend of his owne in such a publick employment, & this prodigall Pope can find none to employ vpon the *penitus toto divisos orbe Britannos.* If he go, rest *a.* confident he shall be armed with *instructions* fro n hence to your mind, & besides you must know I shall haue a great strok with him, for I know how to wield the ressorts that gouern him. But keep this to your self. I am labouring to get such a declaration from the *Pope,* as you desire, in an interim, for your *Dean & Chapter,* & for the *Arch Priests Facultys* to you till all be setled: & I am not out of hope of obtaning it. I make it my owne proposition (not to engage you, in case I should be refused) & will make this Court beholding to me, *b.* to get you to accept it. Therefore be sure you keep your own secret, that if I should be refused yon may

disclaime

a. In all beginnings of negociation he promises much; but in processe performes little Parturiunt montes, nascitur mus.

disclaime me, & not seeme to go lesse in your just requi- *b. Still mag-*
sitions. This court is inwardly much displeased *c.* (though *nificent pro-*
they must not shew it) with some of our *English* asking *mises. But*
their directions how to gouern themselues about the *Oath* , *where is the*
& propositions. For this engageth them to make some de- *effect?*
claration (which yet they will avoyde if they can) aginst
what is both lawfull, & fit, (& so conceiued here) for vs *c. When he*
to do in *England*, as matters stand. But they here must not *saw reasons*
declare a publick allowing of what will be of huge conse- *faile to shew*
quence to the retrenching of their owne pretences elsewhere. *the Lawfull-*
They would haue bin glad it had bin don without asking *nesse of acting*
leaue : & then if there appeare a necessity for them to take *independantly*
notice of it, they would haue seemed to be vnsatisfyed at it, *of Rome, he*
& so haue letten it fall, without doing any thing. In deede *endeavors to*
they all condemne our discretion in not seing this : which *persuade it is*
they did before hand plainly enough intimate to all of vs, *the desire of*
& warne vs not to engage them in a matter, that of one *that Court we*
side myght force them to do what would be odious a brode, *should do so.*
or on the other would be prejudiciall to themselues at home.
This was singly by Fa. *Rector's* worke : who is so stitick, so
formall, & so hidebound, that he is very vnfit for any pru-
dentiall charge. I must do F. *Iohn* & F. *Courtney* this ryght,
that they are mainly for doing what is proposed, & reqvired
of vs, & do publickly declare themselues so, & haue written discourses to mantaine it. But they neede not to convince
the prudent *Cardinalls*, & *Prelates* here : for they avow where
they may be confident, that they haue the same sentiments
herein, as we haue ; but withall say it is not fit for them to
declare so much. There haue beene severall Congregations
about this matter, & they last very long, many hours at a
time, & are kept myghty secret.

You are not well informed of P. *Giles* interest & power
among *English Catholicks*: He gouerneth wholy Mr. *Modtagu*,
but that of late he seemeth to allow a greater liberty to what
we may do, then Mr. *Montagus* devotion will digest. Besides
he gouerneth all the Ambassadors negociation for *Catholicks*,

and

and hath a great hand with severall of the Army & Parliament, & hath treated often with them, by order of the Ambassador, Mr. *Montagu*, my Lord Marques of *Winchester*,
my Lord *Brudenall*, & the *King* himself, & hath gon severall
times between the *King*, & the Ambassador, (all with great
secrecy) in this businesse. He is well affected to vs, & hath
not bad principles of Judgment. But he would fain haue his
Bishoprick dispatched, & till then will not displease this court.
It is now resolved on, & the *Breise* for his Consecration is
speedily intended to be sent to your *Nuntio*: vpon which he
is to come to reside in *France*. I pray you be sure to do him
no prejudice in his owne private pretensions: but make vse
of what I tell you to haue your eyes open. But take no notice to any body else: & know that I shall be able to steere
him to all that is fit.

Card. *Capponi* hath answered your Letter, & I haue sent
them to you a Post, or two a gone. Your Postscript shews
cleerely how much it importeth vs not to trifle in giving
the state satisfaction of our fidelity vnto it, without such a
blind dependance on a despotick Authority of theirs, as is
conceived. For Gods Loue let no time be lost in our doing
our vtmost endeavours to root out that misconceit. Truly
it is vndutifully don of our *Iesuits Rector* in regard of the
Queen, as well as imprudently in regard of all our *Catholicks*
to moue such a businesse of state of his owne head, without
acquainting her Majestys ministers with it. I haue not else
to trouble you with, but rest
Your humble & faithfull servant

Ken. Digby

On the back: To Mr. Fitton 25. nou. 1647.

Sir

❖❖❖❖❖❖❖❖❖❖❖❖❖❖❖❖❖❖❖❖❖❖❖❖❖❖❖❖❖❖❖❖❖❖

Rome 13. Ian. 1648.

Sir *Epiſt.* 38.

As a feauer welcomed me to *Rome*, ſo it vſhereth me out. But Doctor *Fonſeca*, & *Gio. Giacimo* (Mr. *Fitton's* acquaintance) put me in hope, that vppon once or twice Letting bloud & two purges more then what I haue made already, I ſhall be well. Howeuer I will ſet out, though in a litter, aſſoone as I haue the anſwer of the *congregation*, that ſate cloſe on fryday & is to ſit againe this weeke vppon our affaires. If at leaſt they will giue me any anſwer, for I haue ſo put them paſt excuſes, that in truth they can giue me no rationall anſwer (as I heare moſt of the Cardinalls do declare) but doing what I deſire : And that the *Pope* cannot find in his hart to do, for it will coſt him mony, & will juſtify the exiſtence of a ſociety of honeſt men , that will not be fit for this courts ſordide & impious ends. Nether my head , nor hand ſerue me well to write now : Therefore for more particulars I referre you to Sir *Iohn VVintour*, who will haue ſeene my Letter to my Lord *Iermin*. And ſo I reſt

Your moſt obliged & entire ſervant
Ken. Digby.

My harty reſpects to Mr. *Fitton*. If I were out of this accurſed ayre, & vexatious buſineſſe, I ſhould ſurely be preſently well. Which I haue not beene (not thoroughly well) one ſingle day, ſince I came hither.

On the back. To Dr. Holden 13. Jan. 1648.

Sir

❖✧❖

Sir   *Epist.* 39.

Yester nyght I received yours from *Rouen* of the 24. of the last, 1649. & at the same time this enclosed, but from whence, or whom, I know not. I sent you some letters, & writ vnto you saturday last by the ordinary post for *England*, which I should be very glad to heare you had receiued. At the same time I sent one to Mr. *VVatson*. *a.* I haue little to adde ether concerning your priuate affayres, or the publick occurrences of these parts to what I then signifyed vnto you. I haue nothing to say to your kind expressions, but that I should be infinitly glad to be assured of your safe arriuall.

I suppose you will know before this come to your hands that Dr. *Leybourne* went ouer hence from our *English court* well furnished with monys by them, & with order, & instruction *b.* to hinder the *Priests*, & *Catholicks* of *England* not only from obliging, or engaging themselues to any subiection or fidelity to the present state of *England*; but even from receiving any favour from the *Independants* in matters of Religion. To fortify & strengthen his person, & power in this businesse, he hath procured my Lord of *Calcedon* to make him his *Vicar General* ouer all *England*, *c.* which my Lord hath given him by Patent. What dangers may hence follow both to *Religion* in generall, & to the *Clergy* in particular, *d.* you may easily imagin. Mr. *Fitton*, Mr. *Car*, & others here are extreamely offended at this vnfortunat accident. To prevent the future mischeife which will infallibly follow this weake mans ambition thus employed, you may do well not to open your mouth of it, to any *Catholicke*, saue only in common termes (for your freedome of speech *e.* ruins all your affayres)

and

a. This *Watson* was I think Scout master *General* to Cromwel, *a great Confident with the* Blackloists.

b. This is not tru: he had nether Commission, *nor* Instruction from the English Court. Yet this is sayd to set all the Rebels on his back.

and advise secretly with Mr. *VVatson f.* what course to take to haue him at least sent back by the state. He was sent into *Ireland*, he was always on the *Presbiterian* faction, *g.* & a professed enemy to the *Independants*, & a cheife author of all those horrid & wicked reports, which ran current here against your self, Mr. *VVatson*, Mr. *Fitton*, & I as causers of the *King's* death, & as labourers to submit the *Catholicks* of *England* to the *Independant Government* I feare you will find Mr. *Montagu* infected by Mr. *Leybourne's* informations, bringing him Letters from the court here to perswade his concurrence with him: I doubt not but if Mr. *VVatson* be ryghtly informed in the businesse, he will easily do vs all that ryght as to procure meanes to prevent the harmes which this factious & proud spirit *h.* will effect. If those who now gouerne be informed of him, I feare they will not think his returne in the way of banishment sufficient: & therefore I wish the busines were discreetly *i.* managed, & aboue all things that nothing be obiected against him for Religion, *k. that whatsoever he suffer, it may be as a spy, a brouillon, & a factious fellow.* But you will over do this, if you meddle in it your self, & I pray therefore go along with Mr. *VVatson* in the managing of it, & nether appeare your self, *l.* nor any other, but such as are ministers of the publick affayres. I haue often repented my self (for I must tell you all I think) that I gaue you (against the dictamen of my owne Judgment) the paper of the *Catholick Government* in *England* in my owne hand writing, *m.* for you can nether hould your tonge, nor your hand. We heare your stay was long in *Diep* by reason of danger by Sea. And though I feare not your security once landed, *n.* yet I shall not be fully quiet in mind, vntill I heare from you, & of your safe aboad at *London.* Let not Mr. *VVatson o* hasten to fast ouer, let these vehement streames of men's Passions be a little allayed: for one told me this day to my face, that had he beene here at the news of the *Kings* death, *p.* she would haue helped to haue stoned him. Adieu.   Yours as you know   H. H.

Nothing

c. This is tru.

d. How strangely solicitous was the Cabal for their cause, & to secure their footing in the Chapter when they could not endure one Orthodox man should be employed by their Bishop!

e. Medice cura teipsum. VVhat freedom Dr. Holden gaue to his tong, & pen appearres by his Letters, & discourse.

f. You see his Goodwill to a Prime clergy man, & their viçar Generall.

q. Al this is false Dr. Leybourne neuer joyned with Presbiterians, or any Rebels. Nothing written vpon the back anciently. And though it hath no date, yet I beleive it was written before that of the 24. of March, because this accuses Dr. Leybourne of having a commißion from the Queen & that other retracts it. It was written a while after the Execution of his Late Majesty.

h. This is the full intent of these bloudy informations: to preuent all oppofition to the Faction. *i.* He sees these informations may coft Dr. Leybourne more then banishment. *k.* Here is an Idea of the present Persecution: we may think (this present feuere Persecution being a copy of what is here fuggefted) that fome difciple of this man aßifted in the Contriuance of it. *l.* Thus hauing throwne a ftone which myght dash out the Doctor's braines, he hides his hands: that he may feeme to haue done nothing. *m.* If the paper be good & fuch as all Catholicks are bound to confent to, why was he affrayde it should be feen? If it be bad, why did he compose it, & shew it to Parlament men? *n.* VVe shall find hereafter, that notwithstanding all this assurance grounded on their compliance with the Independants, Sir K. D. could find no safety in England: for as Sir K. writes on the 31. Aug. 1649. vpon his arrival at London, he was ordred by the Parliament to depart the nation within twenty days, & not to returne without Leaue vpon pain of death, & confiscation of his Eftate. *o.* How folicitous the good man is for the safety of that Cromwellian! *p.* Henc it appeares that this Letter was writeen a while after that execrable Parricide committed by Rebels on the Perfon of their King.

✦✦✦✦✦✦✦✦✦✦✦✦✦✦✦✦✦✦✦✦✦✦✦✦✦✦✦✦✦✦✦✦✦✦✦✦

Mr. Dr. Holden to Sir Ken. Digby.

Paris the 24. of March 1649.

Sir

Epift. 40.

a. He spares not Sir K. D. you fee. I haue little to anfwer to yours of the 19. but that I am glad you haue receiued the letter you mention, & I wifh you would make good vfe of what I writ concerning your freedome of fpeech *a.* if you knew what prejudice it is to you

you, & what is fayd of it, you would be more carefull. What I writ of Dr. *Leybourne* b. is moſt certain, that is, for his Vicarſhip to my Lord of *Chalcedon* for his commiſſion from the *Queen*, c. that is fayd, but cannot be certainly known, but from himſelf, or thoſe who gaue it him, who I ſuppoſe can hold their Peace. Howeuer becauſe I am certain he will be doing, it were fitt his buſie head were preuented. Mr. *VVatſon* hath ſufficient information of him, d. but I know not whether he will act in ſuch a buſineſſe, vnleſſe he be dealt withall by word of mouth. In the Letter I ſent to you, to *London* (as ſuppoſing you would be there as ſoone as it) there was nothing of conſequence, nor any Letters from ıtaly, for here they are. Monſieur *La Mague* hath received none of yours. Mr. *More* will let you haue 40. piſtols vpon my ſcore. For your negociation in England, I will hope well, nor can there be any hazard in them, ſaue only by too much freedome with one, or the other party, for nether the Catholicks, nor the *Independants* (if they ſettle) muſt know the meanes you intend to ſet on foote, to effect what you may declare to be your deſigne, as being juſt in it ſelf, & contenſull to both ſides, I meane an aſſurance of the Catholicks Fidelity to the common wealth, they are to liue vnder. I cannot ſend you any news of our Engliſh court, for I never enquire after it. Mr. Fitton muſt do it. I beleive your paſſage by Calis would be much more ſecure for the Sea: but by Land I know not.

I will ſend this morning to Mr. *Ferrier*. Our Deputyes are ſtill treating, & are to continew vntill fryday. I much feare we ſhall haue no Peace. All your freinds here ſalute you. Adieu   Yours as ever   H. H.

Nothing written ancienly vppon the back.

are hands of Eſau, *though they affect* Jacob's voice.
                            moſt

Marginal notes:

b. He had been ſent into England by the Biſhop of Calcedon, as his vicar Generall-

c. Here he retracts what he had written in the forgoing Letter.

d. By this hint we may ſee what good offices were done by the Cabál for Dr. Leybovrne a prime officer of the Secular Clergy. By which we may gueſſe what fauours ſuch men, as Regulars may expect from their hands: which

Most *honoured Sir*   *Epist.* 41.

I receiued one from you without date of time or place.
But to giue it satisfaction my residence is at the *Hague.* My
businesse at the present *Geometry* whereof I intend to set
forth some few resolutions to whet the printers appetites

a. This had a
qhite contrary
effect, for the
demonstrated
faults of his
Geometry
proued evi-
dently his
Divinity
was stuft
with like
or worse
errours, seing
he aduises his
Reader by
that writing
to Iudge of
this.

a. to my Divinity, which as yet will not goe downe with
them. I pray God I find meanes to continue vntill I can
perfect it. I write with these a letter to Mr. *Du Bose* to gett
some monyes b. to hold out these hard dayes, for my Inke
freezeth in my pen. I perceiue well I grow old, yet must
I loose time euen against my will wanting mony, & being
put to shift to get some. I haue a project to get monys
from Mr. *du Bose,* but it wil be Easter first, and I doubt
whither I can expect soe long, or no. As for your opinion
of the Blessed Sacrament, if it please God to make vs meete,
we shall discourse to the purpose, then I shall vnderstand
your grounds: & if I can get my Divinity to the presse,
peradventure you will see my intention the better therein.
I am wondrous glad of your good health of body, & minde,
though Dr. *Holden* bee not soe credulous of this last, c. I
meane of the strength you promise your self, & wishing
you all happinesse I rest this 21. of Dec.

Your most affectionate & humble seruant

Tho. White.

b. One point
of most of his
Letters, is
this, want of mony.
whom did he spare?

On the back: from Mr. White 21. Dec. 1649.

c. It seemes Dr. Holden *did not spare Sir K. & indeed*

I haue

❖❖❖❖❖❖❖❖❖❖❖❖❖❖❖❖❖❖❖❖❖❖❖❖❖❖❖❖❖❖❖❖❖❖❖❖

Most honored Cosin.   *Epist.* 42.

I haue sent a letter to the post for you. And since my doing so, I haue receaued that which you haue don me the honour of writing me on thursday, your 7 of this month. I am infinitely oblidged to you for the frendly care you are pleased so nobly, and so charitably to take of my interests. And am ashamed of the troubles I so continually cause you. But I see your goodnesse is not to be wearied out.

I concur with you in all that you say in this letter, and professe my self to haue the same sentiments you so judiciously expresse. So that your writing this to one as supposing me to be of a different opinion, and consequently, your endeavouring to persuade me hereby (for my good) to be of yours, sheweth I haue not in my former letters clearly expressed my selfe: And therefore I will make bold to say a little now imediatly and directly to what is the subiect of this letter of yours. My other letter of this morning seemeth vnto me to say somwhat to this tenor: and I think that most of my former ones do continualy inculcate the vnhappinesse of my condition, that to saue me and children from staruing, did cast me vpon courses and imployments which I forsaw would cause exceptions against me. This I would haue prevented, If I could but haue had means otherwise to liue. But being thrown vpon these rockes, I could not auoyde *a.* hearing some-times things that went much against my Nature, and saying others that being malevolently interpreted myght cause ill odor of me, & complying for outward decency with persons whose ends I no ways concurred with. For all these things I humbly beg a fauourable construction. And do beseech those who shall looke vpon my life and actions, to consider the main bulke of them, and the actiue part of them, and what effects haue resulted out of them; And by these

a. Guesse by this how zelously he serued the Queen, who employed him.

thefe to judge of my intentions; And according to my intentions (which haue euer been fincere & cordiall to the ftate) to ground their opinion of me. If in any thing through indifcretion I haue giuen caufe of miftaking me, or that through error of Judgment I haue fallen into any error, fo as offence may haue been taken at it (which I proteft was euer far from my intention) I do in moft fubmiffiue manner beg indulgence & remiffion, & that it may be gratioufly paffed by : And (let me borrow one further expreffion of the Papiftes doctrine) If I haue, in running through fo may ftraights & neceffities & rockes, committed venial fin, I craue pardon for it, & that long & heavy Purgatory for fo many years may be deemed fufficiently expiatory for it. But as for mortal fin. I will craue no pardon for fuch. They admitt none. They muft proceed from a depraued & averfed minde from the ftate : fuch a one, as is not capable of fauour & mercy : And vpon which nothing but death & ruine ought to follow. For thefe it is that I ftandfo peremptorily vpon my juftification. And which if I fhould admitt but a poffibility of hauing comitted, by craueing fauour for what I may have don in this kinde, I fhould exclude my felfe from all fauour; for I fhould not deferue the leaft. But for all other frailties, errors of Judgment, miftakes & vnhappineffes that my extreme neceffities & the natures of my Employments haue caft vpon me; as I acknowledg my weakneff to lay me abundantly open to fuch beyond my intention; fo I beg grace & pardon for them. And do humbly befeech the ftate, & thofe it fhall defigne to fift & judge my actions, to looke vpon the effects of them, & to examine if euer any of them were in the leaft manner prejudicial to it; & accordingly to determine of my intentions : and by them to let me ftandor fall. This I direct my folicitor & Councel & Frendes to offer and craue in my behalfe; whiles in the mean time, they put me vpon my rigourous juftification for thefe things which properly deferue the name of crimes. To all which I fhall

euer

euer positiuely plead not guilty. And it muſt be legall proofes only, that can attaint me of theſe. Without ſuch the Law declareth the accuſed perſon innocent.

Ill opinons & auerſions, may be entertained of one for only the formes; which though they puniſh not directly, yet they carry great waight & prejudice with them; & one time or other, before the year be ended they will come home to his dore. So that he is in an vnhapy condition, who liueth vnder them. But I hope my ingenuity & ſubmiſſion in order to the things that may begett them, will preſerue me free from that burthen & misfortune, ſo as (Dear Cozin) you will ſtill honour me with your adviſes, & aſſiſtance, & the good offices of your frends: on which three, I repoſe the good ſucceſs of, my cauſe. And whatſoeuer it be, I reſt with all the greateſt obligation that can be to you; & reſigne my ſelfe entirely to what God ſhall be pleaſed to diſpoſe of it & me, now that I haue vſed all the dilligence that I am aware of (as I conceiue I am bound in my duty to my ſelfe to do) adding this only to be repreſented vnto them who ſhall decide it, that if they relieue me not I am vtterly & irrecouerably ruined; the maine ſtock of an auncient family is deſtroyed: & if they will be ſo good as to preſerue me, they will preſerue one who will employ his life & fortune & all that they ſhall enable him with in their ſeruice. All that I haue written in this letter, I beſeech you repreſent to as many as you can, where it may concerne me: & be pleaſed to order my ſolicitor to do the like vnto others where he ſhall judge it may import: as alſo to inſtruct my councel to make vſe of it in due time & place. As I doubt not but he will do the like with what elſe I write to him, or that you are pleaſed to let him ſee of my writing to you. I beſeech you joyne my humble thanks with your obliging ones, to that noble genleman, who for your ſake did ſo worthily put by the calumnie which would haue been brought vpon the ſtage againſt me. Truly, he is one of the galenteſt generoſeſt

perſons

perfons, I haue euer receiued fouours from. They are all vpon your fcore. Therefore you are in obligation of making high acknowledgments of them. I take vp too much of your time for one poft-day; & the packet-boat is ready to be gon. Therefore remitt vnto my next, the refleêctions I make vpon what you & your Cofin haue Philofophically reafoned. By my two to you of the 19 of this Month, & by my third of the 14 you will perceiue I haue received thofe letters of yours which you mention in this now. But you will haue reafon to fay I haue no mercy, but weary you beyond all limitts of good manners & difcretion. Therefore without further lengthening your troble by making an apology, I humbly take leaue and reft

    Your moft humble and faithfull feruant and
      moft affeêctionate kinfman
           Kenelme Digby

    Loofe not courage for that in my bufineffe you finde fo great difficultes; & that dayly new ones arife; It is the nature of all great bufineffes, to encounter with great difficultes. And this is the greateft I euer had or can haue. All my liuelihood, & future well-being of my whole family dependeth of it. Induftry & patience with Gods bleffing will maftter all. And then, the harder we were put to it, the greater will be our comfort & joye.

                           Sir

Sir K. D. his cafe is not to be confidered barely vpon
the blunt proofes as they lye before the Barons in an ordinary legall courfe (althô euen in that confideration , it
ftandeth fair; fince, punifhments ought not to be inflicted,
but where the crime is evident & vndoubted :) for that were
too narrow a compaffe , for a bufineffe , & a perfon fo much
looked vpon as this has been. Such as thefe are not only
obiects of private Juftice ; but do alfo carry with them the
force of publick examples; whereby the minds & apprehenfions of multitudes of men are quieted & fecured, and
are encouraged to apply their induftries to merit of the ftate;
whofe Juftice & magnanimity (that hath larger & nobler
rules , then do belong to a particular tribunall) is thence
rendred confpicuous & beloued by all men. In this cafe then,
(where the actions in controverfy , haue paffed vpon an e-
minent ftage) the fupreme Judges may pleafe to confider,
1. the time , & the Perfons behaviour before thofe actions;
2ly. The circunftances that he was in, when his behauiour
feemed doubtful. And laftly , his carriage euer fince. The
firft , comprifeth all the time from Sir K. D. his entring into
rhe management of publick affairs , & his comportment in
them , till his going out of England from Winchefter houfe,
by allowance of the Parliament. During all this time his carriage was fuch, as made him be looked vpon as one *a*. endew-
ed with the publicke fpirite of a true Patriote , & averfe to
the byas & private interefts of thofe who were in power &
fwayed in all that feafon ; as may be evidently made to appeare , by many notable examples in his management of the
Nauy , & of the Ordinance ; by fundry actions of his out of
England , & by feverall other Employments at home ; if any
one fhall doubt thereof : But no proofe can be ftronger , then
that in the beginnings of the diftempers between the Parliament

a. Sir K. D.
pretends to
haue been ac-
cufed to the
Court even
before the Ci-
vil wars.

and

4

and the late King, when all thofe who were affected to the
wayes of the Court embarked themfelues in the interefts of
it. Yet he behaved him felfe fo, that at his going then out
of England, when he was allowed the honour of taking leave
folemnely of the Parliament he received from it the greateft
demonftration of kindneſs & the moſt obliging civilities, that
it euer did to any private perſon; & withall, declared him
innocent of all crimes that he ftood accuſed of againſt the
ftate (for euen then, there wanted not fome few who were
adverfe vnto him) & ordered him the quiet poſſeſſion of his
eftate, & gaue him licence to carry ouer what he pleafed of
his goods; as may be feen in the Regifters of the Orders
of both Houſes then.

For the 2. Confideration; They may pleaſe to be informed
how his vnhappineſs was fuch, that he was no fooner gone
out of England; but fome of the country committies who

b. He pre-
tends, that
he was fent
to Rome by
the Queen of
France, then
Regent. How
tru this pre-
tence is, let
the world
judge.

were not rightly poſſeſſed vpon what faire termes he went
a way, but vnderftood his departure as a baniſhment, and
fwayed by popular Rumers, & took advantage of his abfence
fequeftred his eftate: fo that he had not wherewithall to fub-
fift abroad; & to maintaine his 3 fons that he had by him then
in France. Herevpon he often petitioned both houfes, expreſſing the diftreffed condition he was in, & befeeching leave
to returne and juftifie him felfe of any crime might be ob-
jected againſt him, or receive puniſhment in his perfon as
well as in his eftate if he fhould be found guilty. But the
great affairs of the Parliament could never allow the leafure
to take his petition into confideration. Wherevpon he wrot
feverall letters to fome of the eminenteft Members of both
houfes, to acquaint them with the extreme neceffity & exigents
he was in, & wih what was propofed to him to giue him
meanes of fubfiftance; namely an Employment (the myfte-
ries whereof, & the reafons of pitching vpon him, he has
informed feverall of the Parliament) for France *b*. (but
vnder the Queen of Englands name) to Rome: which he
was

was very vnwilling to accept of; fearing the mifconftructions at home that might follow fuch an Employment. thô he was refolved and certain that in it he fhould do nothing in effect that was vnfit for a faithfull fervant *c.* of the ftate. Thus, extreme neceffity, to be able to live himfelfe, and to give his Children bread, forced him (after frequent advertifments thereof at home, to deliver him of it, if it might be) to engage him felfe in that Employment which is the only thing that hath begoten any doubt concerning him : Infine, fuch a neceffity, as ever by the law of Nature & of Nations, alloweth a man to take by violence, to break open doors, to fteale food to keep himfelf & children alive when they are ready to ftarue. And yet the heavieft accufation againft him layeth not to his charge, any particular negotiation wherein he may haue deferved ill of the ftate (which certainly would haue broken out to light in this long time; if he had acted in any) but only fufpitions arifing from a third perfons letter, written in generall terms, & vpon God knoweth what particular defignes of his owne; & from the courfe he was in, which he could not avoyde : And which the rather cleareth the candor of his minde towardes the ftate; fince in fuch difficult circumftances, he behaved himfelfe fo as nothing rifeth to beare evidence againft him.

 The laft & moft important confideration of all is how Sir K. D. hath behaved himfelfe euer fince his leaving to walke in thofe myfty paths, that afforded fome ground for fufpition. In which it is to be obferved that as foon as he had fetled a correfpondence betweene France & the .Court of Rome to which he was employed, he prefently came away from thence. If thofe interefts which are contrary to this ftates interefts, had carried him thither; they would ftill have kept him there, for they dayly preffed more and more. But as foon as a French Ambaffador was fettled there, he prefently returned : which maketh it cleare that his employment was but in order to that, & to the confequences
      thereof

c. He was then refolued to be very faithfull to the Q. who employed him

thereof. As foon as he had giuen an account of his employment to the King & Queen of France that fent him (as they themfelues do witnefs) he continued his former induftries to haue leaue to returne home, to juftifie himfelfe, or vndergo any fevere punifhment if he fhould be found guilty of any objeƈted crime. It was then an aƈtive & bufy time with the ftate of England; which caufed, that few private bufineffes could be heard; & among others, his had no anfwer. Wherevpon he came over himfelfe into England, to encounter all that could be objeƈted againft him, without any proteƈtion or fecurity at all, but what his Innocence & a cleare Confcience could give him.

Whiles he was there, all, that he petitioned for, was to be heard, to have fevereft Judges examine his caufe, & to afford him nothing of Grace, but bare Juftice. He was *d.* commanded away, not for any thing imputed againft himfelfe, but for fufpitions accafioned by others behaviour; which now fince, by traƈt of time (that bringeth darkeft matters to light) appeareth to haue had no folid reflexion vpon him. But he hath ftill continued by his fon & neereft friends, to preffe for Juftice, & to be brought to further punifhment if he deferve it. In the mean time he hath been expofed to all the fufferances, dangers & extremities, that want & diflike of thofe, neere whom he hath been forced to live, haue caft him vpon. Adde to thefe, invitations that cannot faile of having been offered to a perfon whofe parts & experience in the world are fufficiently known. Yet all this hath not begot any impatience in him, nor tempted him to fteere any other courfe, nor made him flack in endeavouring to do very important fervices to the ftate (as feverall in the Parliament do know very particularly) And, for a plenary proofe & evidence of this candor & integrity to the ftate; they all know that during thefe 5 years that he hath been returned from Rome, in which time fo many difcoueries have been made of the clofeft mens darkeft tempers & defignes,

by

d. VVhere was that credit of which he boafted whileft he was in Rome with the Prime Independants.

by the taking of so many papers, by the surprifing & examining of so many of their Enemies Agents, & particularly now at the vpfhot of all by the perufall of all the King of Scots papers, & of all his fecreteft frends letters to him, from his firft entrance into affairs to this laft attempt) taken at Jerfey; Not the lefte fhadow appeareth of any thing to be fufpected e. in Sir K. D. which is an argument of fo great an Innocence & integrity & foundnefs of hart in him as bloweth away & cleareth any mift of fufpition that vpon any doubtfull action of his, long fince done, may be raifed againft him.

Therefor, vpon the whole matter; fince acts of ftate in punifhing eminent perfons, are to be looked vpon rather as publike medicines & examples for the future, then as expiations for particular offences paft long agoe, (which is too narrow a confideration for the fupreme body of a great ftate) certainly it belongeth to the maieftie & honorablenefte of fuch a noble ftate as that of England, to pafs generoufly over fuch few dark fteps of his life as neceffity did long fince caft him vpon, & that peradventure fome narrow & fcrupulous natures might a while ftick at; And refolue to make vfe (fome way or other) of the tallents of fuch a perfon, as all men know hath been in a courfe that may haue enabled him to be ferviceable to his f. country; Or at leaft to allow him to live quietly & retiredly vnder the protection of the ftate, which he has been fo induftrious to ferve (and with no fmall hazard to himfelfe) as feverall in the houfe do know Sir K. D. hath been. This proceeding will win the affections of multitudes, g. when they fhall fee that, even in doubtfull cafes, a good temper of their minds will draw vpon them the benignity & favour of the ftate; & that all men are not expofed indifferently to the lafh & feuerity of the laws but that the ftate is fo generous as to make fauorable conftructions of fuch enforced actions as the neceffity of broken times haue caft well-meaning men vpon

e. This proueth, that the Royal Party had little efteeme of Sir K. D.

f. He hath a great efteeme of of his owne parts as alfo Blacklo. But I think nobody elfe efteemed him.

g. He thinks the world much concerned for his eafe: fo a boy who fold matches in Paris folling into the Seine, & being in danger of drowning fayd, what wil becōe of Paris if I am drowned ?

vpon, to keep themfelves aliue in a ftorme ; which admitteth not a regularity in euery piece of a mans behaviour : It will fettle many wavering harts: It will fecure & quiet many mens fears : And in a word, it wi'l worke a like effect in the ftate of England, as the abfoluing of Fabius Maximus did in the Romane ftate ; which is fo judicioufly obferved by one of the wifeft hiftorians that ever was, in thefe words : *Non minus firmata eft Refpablica Romana Periculò Quinti Fabÿ Maximi, quam fupplicio miferabili Titi Manlÿ.* The freeing of men (who have merit or ability to plead for them) from punifhment, in doubtfull cafes ; conduceth as much to the fetling of the laws & Juftice in a cōmon wealth, as the puifhing of guilty perfons.

If there fhould be any claufe in the exceptions of the Act of Oblivion, that may poffibly be contrued to reach me (in cafe my bufinefs be not ended before it come out) Methinketh it fhould be a very good ground for my frends to move the Parliament in my behalfe, that when fo many thoufands of delinquents are made happy by the grace and pardon of the ftate, it doth not fuit with their high goodnefs & noblenefs & gentlenefs, to let a perfon remaine in want & miferie & all kinds of difcomfort (through fome cafual fhortnefs of the act of Oblivion in his particular) that hath fhewed fo much conftant affection to the ftate; And is therefore looked vpon with great animofity by the enimies of the ftate.

Paris 27. March. 1652.

In Mine of the 20. I fent you the heads of fuch confiderations as I conceave are moft important for my frends in the houfe to reflect vpon ; who, as being the judges of my caufe, are to confider & fpeake of it in a higher ftraine and

and vpon nobler & larger principles, then belongeth to Advocates or lawyers in a plaine way; who attend only to what is pofitively proved in that precife caufe which they plead in; without looking fo far to thé confequences & dependance of it, & to the Rules of Generofity that belongeth to a ftate or to a King. For I make account, that the Senate of Rome (vnto which ours now is conformable) or Julius, or Auguftus Cefar; were fwayed, in cafes pleaded before them, by other & hygher notions, then fuch as were to gouerne the private Tribunals vnder them.

Paris 30. March. 1652.

I have no more to adde concerning my bufinefs, but that you put my agents in remembrance of a confideration I have often writ vnto them; which I conceave is one of the importanteft & moft mouing ones to get me a good dimiffion of my feqveftration, that can be vfed. And it will come feafonably in, at the clofe & winding vp, after the juftice of my cafe hath been made to appeare by fome frends fpeaking in my behalfe in the houfe. And it is; to reprefent to the ftate that in freeing me of delinquency, & in taking of the fequeftration of my eftate, they relinquifh nothing that they already haue; nor do giue me, or part with ought that they have poffeffion of, or can ever be in away or poffibility to poffefs, but by firft enabling me to be owner of it. For, my eftate is now out in mortgage, & engaged for other debts that muft fucceede the mortgage; fo that nothing will be to come to me (and confequently not to the ftate neirher) in 20. years, & more, if it be let lye as it is. And all this while they haue no tye vpon my good behaviour; for, whatfoever I fhould do or attempt, I can be in no worfe cafe then I am; Whereas fetting me vpright. And vpon faire termes with

the

the world, they will put me in a condition to make me vse induſtry to recover what I can of my eſtate, & to pay my debts vpon better aduantage then to let them eate themſelues our ; And my Mother will do ſomething for me, when I may be better for it. And thus the ſtate will haue a ſolide tye (of ſome conſiderable fortune) vpon me, to oblige me to duty & reſpectful behaviour to them, as well as the motiues of affection and honeſty in me.

On the back : Reflections vpon my caſe for ſome of my freinds in the houſe. Sent to my Coſ. Digby, & my ſon 20. 27. & 30. March 1652. All in Sir K. D.'s hand.

This Letter is not printed in the order of its date ; but after that other of the 21. Feb. 1650. It being a further explanation of it.

❖❖❖❖❖❖❖❖❖❖❖❖❖❖❖❖ ❖❖❖❖❖❖❖❖ ❖❖❖❖❖❖❖❖❖❖❖

Sir K. D. to Monſieur Du Boſe.

Sir   Epiſt. 43.

I cannot forbeare writing to you ; & yet I know not what to ſay. Such is the effect of extream greifes , that they can neither be ſilent, nor ſpeake to the purpoſe. In a letter yeſterday from Mr. Holden I received newes of the tragicall accident befallen in your family ; which almoſt ſtrucke me dead too. Beleive me, Sir, I beare a great ſhare in the exceſſive greife, you moſt needes haue vpon this occaſion. As ſoone as I could recover my ſelfe out of my aſtoniſhment, I betooke my ſelfe preſently to ador his Providence that keepeth an exact account of every hayre of our head , & without

without which not a sparrow falleth to ground. In a deepe & entire resignation vnto that, is al the comfort we can find in such bitter stroakes. I wish you as many helps, & as great & true ones as I can to my owne hart. But least I should be importune to you, holding you too long with my broken sighes, I will turne them from you to God Almyghty in your behalfe; who only can giue ease to your Iust sorrow. Whiles I shall haue a deepe sense of all that concerneth you, & shall euer be

  Sir   your most humble & most faithfull seruant
         Kenelme Digby

Calais the 9. Feb. 1650.

On the back: To Monsieur Du Bose, when his son killed his owne sister (that was with child) & then himselfe.

❀❀❀❀❀❀❀❀❀❀❀❀❀❀❀❀❀❀❀❀❀❀❀❀❀❀❀❀❀❀❀❀❀❀❀

Sir K. D. to Mr. Blacklovv

       Calais 25. Feb. 1652.

Most hononred Sir   *Epist.* 44.

Your letter of the 21. Decem. appeared to haue made a circuit about, for it was of an old date before I received it. And it hath layne longer by me: for I made account every weeke to haue from *England* meanes to answere it better then by bare acknowledging the receipt of it. But it is Gods will, that when my desire is strongest & my owne neede, & my best frendes most vrging, I should then be most destitute & forsaken. You would not easily beleive what distresses & wants I have endured here, even in such necessary thing, as
             a person

a perfon living in the world, cannot well be without. His bleſſed name be prayſed forit. My Mother aſſiſteth me what ſhee is able. But ſhee is in apittiful ſad condition her ſelfe: God helpe her. My frendes in England bid me hope for a ſpeedy releiſe out of my eſtate. But as yet it cometh not. And there is great animoſity againſt me. I do what I can, & vſe all the Art & Dexterity, I am capable of, to become maſter of ſome thing, that I may tranſplant it among *Chriſtians*. But the tyde runneth ſtrong againſt me. Yet I am confident, that with patience, & with conſtant & ſteady vſing thoſe induſtryes I purſue, I ſhall bring my buſineſſe to a reaſonable iſſue. In the meane time I ſuffer not a little. I thank God my doing ſo is not the leaſt trouble, or affliction to my minde. Nor, in regard of my ſelf ſingly, would I caſt away one bare howers thoughts, or care to remedy it all. But I conceive it is my duty to vſe thoſe diligences I doe: for I ſee very great goods that I myght ſet on foote, & advance, if I had my owne transferred into theſe partes. God hath bin very mercifull to me in weaning me by little, & little & in proceſſe of time, & by an admirable providence, (that I can reade plainely in the great variety of accidents which have befallen me) from all deſires, & affection to the world : not by a deepe melancholy, vpon any ſharpe misfortune, as once before, which made onely the preſent face of things become diſpleaſing to me; but by a through Change of my taſte : *a.* not wrought of a ſuddaine; but after many viciſſitudes in a long courſe of time, vpon mature, & deepe conſideration of the emptineſſe, & vnſatisfyingneſſe of preſent, & fading goods, & of the reality & fullneſſe of future ones. I long to be, where I may be inſtructed by you at leiſure, & att full of theſe things : for I beleive I am growne more capable of them, then you have ever yet kuowne me to be: I find in my ſelf the powerfull effects of *ſolitude*, & *ſilence*: which I enjoyed (vpon the matter) now above a yeare. In which time they have much ripened the ſeedes, that have bin

a. Here are good diſpoſitions to vertu, if he had fallen vpon an orthodox, & able Inſtructer.

bin long fowed, & flowly growing in me. For though I
have bin often obliged to negociate my bufineffe with others
(& other conuerfation then fuch I have avoyded, & have
not had) yet that hath not at all flackened or layed a fleepe
my love of retirement. But rather hath much encreafed it,
by reafon of the difpleafingneffe, & vncouthneffe of fuch employments. Thofe only which be pleafing ones, do endanger the relenting, or eneruing of ones minde. Yet withall
the diftaftfull buſying of ones thoughts doth beget a diforder
in ones foul, which hindreth it from being efficacious in
good, though it win it not to a compleafance in what is bad.
So that befides my naturall incapacity & weakeneffe, the duft
that is rayfed in me by irregular motions of bufineffe hindreth me from aduancing much, though through the mift
of it I defcry which way my Journy lyeth. *Paciencia con la*
Paz (that *Gregory Lopez* fo much recommendeth, & that I
hope I am not farre from being in a condition to be able to
enjoy) will affuredly allay the one, & in the' other I promife my felfe a happy betterment by your charitable helpe.
What may be done at a diftance, cannot be (I confeffe)
fo efficacious there vnto, as what I fhall learne from you
when we may *notas audire & reddere voces*. Yet in the meane
time I will beg of you to fett downe in writing fome fuch confiderations, as you who know my palate, & grounds (as having
formed the one in me, & given me the other) may judge will be
profitable & mouïg to me. Without fuch I fhould, not lye, if I
fayd, that your redeeming me out of vulgar ignorance, hath bin
in fome regard a misfortune to me : As the cure of madneffes
was to the poore wretch, who then faw his mifery, whereas
before he lived contentedly, fo your vnfieling my eyes hath
rendred thofe motives of Devotion, & Charity which worke
ftrongly vpon others. Moft vnfavoury, & flat to me, and
fuch as will by no meanes downe with me. The only way to
releieve me out of this diftreffe, is to give me folid & tru ones. I
acknowledge I am not altogether vnprovided of fuch from you.

But

But I would be glad to have a compleate body of Considerations & Meditations vpon weyghty and subsisting groundes, to rayse a strong love of the *Vnum necessarium*, & a prime and close adhesion to it. When I reade in the spirituall bookes I meete with, *b.* how pleasing some actions are to God almyghty, how displeasing others: how he punisheth these, how he rewardeth the others: how the merits, & price of Christs passion is to be applyed to vs, how strict a Judge he will be, how materiall actions, & *opera operata* do cancell sins, & encrease Grace, & what they describe Grace to be, I grow froward, & am rebutted with Devotion, instead of being inflamed, as they intend it. Such discourses as vsually dry spirituall masters are stuffed with, do move me as much, as Rhombus his Mocke-oration in Sir Philip Sidry's entertainment of the Queen (as intended by a foolish Pedant, for a paterne of Eloquence) did move the hearers. Yet I acknowledge that all they say of positiue doctrine is tru: but God knoweth it is tru in a quite other sense, then as they afterwards explicate it. They vnfold these hygh, & excellent Mysteryes (out of the knowledge whereof resulteth our way to beatitude) in a pittifull low straine, proportionable to their Narrow capacityes, & meane learning. I would have them lively delineated accordingly as truly they are, without any figuratiue speakings, & doctrines grounded vpon the mistaken senses of the words, which in their genuine sense we are bound to beleive. I would be glad to *c.* see the whole oeconomy of Gods making & saving vs, & the considerations that are entayled vpon that (as what he is, who we are, & the like) orderly set downe, in the method of Causes, & effects connaturally relating to one another: & due reflection vpon them, to stirre vp affections, & resolutions in vs. And for a crowne of all, what is to be done on mans part, & what considerations he is at last to fix vpon, to bring himself into a disposition to receive at Gods liberall hand (which is never scanty, where it finds adue preparation) the

gift

b. Here he gathers such opinions as were inspid to his Palate, by reason of the tast, Mr. Blacklo had framed in him. VVhich (opinions) being for the most part taken out of Scripture, & commended therein by the Holy Ghost, it is a blasphemy to vilify or contemne them. He blames, that in spirituall writers, some Actions, are sayd to please God others to displease

gift of contemplation, & of prayer without intermiſſion, that S. Paul recommendeth vnto vs, & that the prodigious *Gregory Lopez* ſo hyghly practiſed. When one tells me barely, you muſt do ſuch an action, beauſe God commandeth it. Or forbeare ſuch a one, becauſe he forbad it, alſo he will be angry with you, & caſt you into Hell, to be tormented by vgly Divils, & burned with fire & brimſtone, & that if you will ſay ſuch prayers, & communicate in ſuch a Church on ſuch a day, you ſhall gaine a plenary Indulgence, & thereby balke Purgatory. I grow ſicke with hearing him, & my head aketh, & I become as one that ſhould ſtand in neede of ſome hygh Cordiall, & a ſilly Phyſitian giveth him ſmall beere to comfort himſelf with. But when one ſheweth & conuinceth me, how no created d. good can ſatisfy, & fill the infinit capacity of the ſoule, & that what aff ctions ſoeuer it goeth out of the body with, e. they remaſe eternally indeleble in it, & that the Activity of aſeparated one is infinitly beyond what is in an imbodyed one, whereby the pleaſure & ſorrow of it becomes vnexpreſſible, then I confeſs, he ſetteth me on fire to learne carefully what affections, & Judgments I am to ſtore my ſelfe with in this world: & he maketh me deſpiſe & hate all the obiects I conuerſe with here, which may hinder me from happineſſe hereafter. When he goeth a little furder, & makes me have ſome glimmering of an infinit good, that will not on'y fill, but infinitly overreach the vtmoſt capacity of the Largeſt intellectuall created nature: In whom the goodneſſe beauty, order, & excellence of all creatures is reſumed in an infinitly hygher ſtraine, then ſhineth in them, and whereof what they have are but faint ſhadows, & ſtreaming from that ſubſtantiall fountaine: To whom all time, place, & Actions are preſent, as flowing in an vnconceivable manner from him, from whom all things that are haue received their being: And that all theſe truths, & that infinit others do ſpring vp in vs from the conſideration of this ſimple ſelfe-Being. And

him. *And why ſhould they not ſay ſo, ſeing God commands ſome, & forbids others, & by conſequence is pleaſed with the firſt, & diſpleaſed with the ſecond? And he puniſheth the later ſort of Actions, & rewardes the former, we reade Mat. 25. And that he is aſtrict Judge, is cleare, for he will exact an account even of every idle word. Mat. 12. 36. That aliqua opera operata, actiõs themſelfes,*

that

cancels sins, & encreafe Grace, is defined in the Council of Trent : & ly them, & our on ne Tupreatural Actions, done in obedience to the Law of God, the Merits & price of Chrift's Paffion is applyed to vs, as we learne from the fame Council. VVhy he fhould loath thefe (which he onnes to be Truths) feing the Holy Ghoft, & the increated wisdome did vfe them, as Motiues to vertu, I cannot fee, but

that our vnderftanding, & foul & Being will be fo enlarged, & ftretched out by this felfe Beeing, & eternall truth, as to become one with it, & be in a manner transformed into it, if we fet our harts entirely vpon it, & make this affection the principle from whence all our actions proceede, & banifh from our commerce all thofe objects that may draw vs an other way. I then grow weary of the wofull, & wretched employments the Earth confines her children vnto, And I become impatient, that I find none to deliver me from the body of this death, & to releafe me out of this prifon, that I may take my flyght to that happy ftate I fee befor me. And this I fay only to give you fome hinte of what it is I would be att, wherein I crave your affiftance, & inftructions. I doubt not, but you haue framed vnto your felfe an entire feries of fuch confiderations; and have at leaft beaten them often in your dayly thoughts. But if you have not as yet committed them to paper, or reduced them to an ordely methode, it will not be time loft to your felfe (whiles it will be a great charity, & contentment to me) that you vouchfafe att my requeft to take your pen now & then (when you have entire leafure, & difpofition of minde for it, & compofe them into Meditations, & divide them into points, and feverall jointes: and fet downe practically thofe particular and familiar rules, which are neceffary for one that intendeth a tru fpirituall life, after an intelligible, & folide manner in the moft efficatious way he can propofe to himfelf, capable of. It may paraduenture feeme vnto you (if I haue not expreffed my felfe well) that I entreate what you have already done, in that excellent treatise you wrote fome yeares agone to me : (which I would to God you would give me leaue to publifh in print for an vniuerfall good) But you fee I haue my thought vpon that whileft I defire this, & therefore you will conceive it is fome thing elfe, which I now defire. That is a compleate & perfect p ece in its kind. But to form a compl ete fpirituall man, it requireth this other be added to it.

That

That anatomiseth thoroughly the theory of what is to be aimed at in a spirituall life, & extendeth to the practicall part likewise in som degree: but it descendeth not to such particulars, as I wish to have, & neede. It leaveth off there, after it addresseth to them in generall. To do this will be no tedious, nor voluminous work. A few considerations well chosen, & well pursued will serue the turne. And a few Rules will be sufficient to practice. In the making of which let me put you in minde of what I have often heard you say in commendation of *Sales* his Introduction, that you judged it the best book hath been written of that kind, because it descendeth to sundry minute practicall directions, which have a great influence vpon ones actions, & which all other writers doe slide over. When you shall take this matter into your thoughts, I beseech you employ them also particularly in composing some meditations for receiving the B. Sacrament, *f.* to instruct one to performe that hyghest action of Christian Religion in such manner, as one may hope to obtaine by it the happy fruit of it. I am now the more emboldened to entreate this Charity of you, because I vnderstand you are ere this or are expected at Doway; where (for the time you designe to stay) your minde will not be so much in suspence, & disquiet about disposing of your selfe, as whiles you were in Holland. I shall be glad to heare from you, of your being there, & how long you are likely to continu so, & how you doe, & are in circumstances to your liking. What *g.* becometh of your Divinity? And what of your Geometricall Propositions, that in your last, you told me you were publishing? I pray you cast now to loose as little time, as you can from the great designe you have projected. And remember the first line of Hyppocrates his Aphorismes: *Ars longa vita brevis.* What cometh of me, you shall heare from time to time. If you be at Doway, I pray remember my respects & seruice to worthy Doctor Hyde. And recommending my selfe to your good prayers

but that his stomack, & Palate was very much disordred, & cut of tast: Otherwise how could these things recorded in scripture, as vsefull to Piety, make him forward, & be rebutted with devotion?

c. VVhat he here desires, viz to see, the Oeconomy of God's making & Saving vs: what he is, what we are, &c, orderly set downe, he may find it orderly set downe in the ſpiritual Exerciſes of S. Ignatius, or any of thoſe others who follow him: & that with ſuch re-flections, as may move vs to imbrace that vnum neceſſariũ, in caſe ryghtly ap-plyed. But all theſe humble, plaine & ſub-ſtantiall Conſidera-

prayers, & craving pardon for my tedious letter, which is ſpun out to this length before I am ware, I reſt

Your moſt affectionate & moſt obliged humble ſeruant & tru frend   Kenelme Digby

Father Clarke at Newport deſireth much you ſhould ſee his Poeme, which he hath now finiſhed, & put his laſt hand vnto it, vnleſſe you cut him out new worke. I write no-thing to you, of Monſieur du Boſe, becauſe I make ac-count Dr. Holden doth all that is requiſite. He is very bare of mony (as we are all at preſent) & hath had lately a very great affliction in the loſſe of his children? And what ſay you to him? Thoſe of his coate ſpeake wonders of him: but you know their geeſe are all ſwans. And by the bulke of his book (as it is deſcribed to me) I ſhould ſuſpect, the Authour is too heauy, & hath too little fire for ſo a very ataske.

On the back: to Mr. White 25. Feb. 1650.

tions, in thoſe workes are faſtidiouſly deſpiſed by the Blackloiſts, as they were in Scripture by the Pagans, both out of a motive of Pride, & of their owne con-tempt of what had not the character of the ſpirit, which animated them. Althô, God knows, of all the conſiderable number of men in the world, the Blackloiſts haue the leaſt reaſon to harbour ſuch diminutiue thoughts of others, who are no ways in-feriour to their beſt, ether in Piety, or Learning. I will ſay nothing of the Diſciples, their maſter himſelf what hath he of his owne beſides ſhamefull errours? VVhat is good in him, is tranſlated from others, & impayred by the tranſlation. He hath printed a ſmall book of Meditations, all borrowed of & to be found in the meaneſt of thoſe Authours, whom Sir K. D. treates ſo contemptibly, except ſome vncharitable (& therefore very vnfit) reflections on Religious vertues ſo that nothing but their ig-norance occaſioned the groundleſſe eſteeme they haue, for that Perſone. Now ſi Lu-men quod in te eſt tenebrę ſunt, ipſæ tenebræ quantæ erunt? If their Doctor be ſo ignorant, what are the Diſciples? If their hygh Cordial be ſuch dead Beere, what is their ſmall Beere. To vſe his compariſon.

That

d. That no created good can fill the capacity of our foul, *is no new thought of* Mr. Blacklo. *S.* Auftin *hath it:* Creafti nos Domine ad te, & inquietum eft cor noftrum donec requiefcat in te. *S.* Bernard, *our foul* Creatis rebus occupari poteft, fatiari non poteft. *Thefe & many fuch are cited by mafters of fpirit, in the contemplation of the love of God: of whom* Mr. Blacklo *Learnt it. The fame I fay of thofe other Confiderations, of the* goodnefs beauty, order, & excellence *of all* Creatures in God, *that Infinit goodnefs, beauty, &c: in all which* Mr. Blacklo *had been in the dark, if he had lyghted his taper at their Torch.*

e. But it is *peculiar to* Mr. Blacklo *that all the foul's affections when* feparated from the body, *remaine indeleble for all Eternity. And that all its torment is to retaine thofe, As he fays, tho he teaches, the foul joys in them, & in all other qualitys, it poffeffes, as much as they difcrue, altho they difcrue more joy, then all this world can afford: this I fay inpeculiar to him, & is fo far from diverting men from vnlawfull affections, that it is no weake incentiue to them. For as Saints Love God, & loue this Loue of God, & defire it may neuer be changed; So wicked men Loue vnlawfull objects, & Loue that Loue, & defire it were perpetuall, & are cooled in their Loue when they think it may be Changed. And were men perfwaded, there was no other Hell, nor other paines in Hell, but to enioy thofe Affections; nor Ioys in Heaven, but to be free from them, I feare many would prefer Hell to Heauen in the life to come, as they prefer finfull affections to thofe which are pious, in this. And I haue knowne fome, who fayd, hauing reade, & weyghed thefe Doctrines:* could I beleive him I would play the Roman, & kill my felf. *Viz, to com fooner to thefe Ioys which he promifes in the world to come, even to profligate finners fo wrary would they be of the body of this death, & fo defirous of that life, which at worft, is better & more happy, then all the joys in this life united can make: & yet they remaine voyd of all Loue of God, or tru vertu.*

f. The receiving of the B. Sacrament, is indeed the hyghest action of Chriftian Religon, *by which we are in fome manner* concorporated *with* Chrift, *as* S. Cyril of Hierufalem *fays in his Catechifme. And our fpiritual writers haue not neglected the difpofitions neceffary for it. And befides that previous, of being free from fin (which* S. Paul *requires by thofe words:* Probet feipfum homo) *they require a* great Faith, *beleiving it to be, what it is, the tru body of Chrift.* 2. Great Humility, *which the Church recommends faying thrice:* Domine nonfum dignus, *when fhee gives the* Communion. 3. Great Charity, *to anfwer that*

that, which Chrift manifefted in the Inftitution *of this Divine Sacrament, giving himfelf to vs. Thefe I fay we find in our fpiritualifts, & what Mr.* Blacklo *ever did fay equall to thefe, if he would fay any thing different from them, I cannot tell.*

g. I beleive it was not long before Sir K. D. knew the Fate *of thofe* Geometrical Propofitions, *which no fooner faw the* Light, *but their deformity being difcovered, they were by their publisher condemned to perpetuall darkneß. And doubtleſſe the fame* Fate attends *the* Divinity *of the fame man: that being a like falfe, (& of a more dangerous nature,) thô it may be a little longer lived, becaufe its Falshood is not fo eafily difcovered.*

❖❖❖❖❖❖❖❖❖❖❖❖❖❖❖❖❖❖❖❖❖❖❖❖❖❖❖❖❖❖❖❖

Sir Ken. D. to Mr. Iacob Boeve.

Moſt VVorthy Sir *Epiſt. 45.*

Your moſt obliging Letter of the 30. of Sept. had a long Journy about: for it went firſt to Paris, & after fome delay there it was fent me hither. So that I received it not till yeſterday. I have written twice to you fince my arrivall here: As being confident you were reſtored fafe to your owne home, fince both Windes, & Seas & all the Elements, & whole Nature her felfe have an intereſt in preferuing fo excellent a perfon, *a.* borne for an vniuerfall good. But now that I reade vnder your owne hand the difficultyes & dangers that God delivered you from in your paſſage, I muſt againe congratulate & rejoice with you for fo fignall a deliverance. And I do pray God you may enjoy long life for the comfort of your freinds, & the benefit of all mankind: for they are not narrow circumfcribed thoughts, that fill your noble breaſt. I would I had the foule of *Æſculapius* in me, to contribute the better to that wifhed end. But fuch poore knowledge as I have acquired by Long experience (& cheifely vpon my felfe) I fhall always moſt readily Sacrifice vnto you.

Now

a. VVhat a fawning hyperbolicall, abominable flattery, have we here.

Now to what you enquire of me in your Letter.

Now Sir concerning the deafenes *b*. of the perfon you write of contracted fome yeares fince by a great cold. I conceive it likely to be fome flegmaticke & vifcus humour, that is congealed & hardned in the paffage of the eare, and fo hindreth the perception there of the ayres motion. I will tell you an eafy & familiar remedy for this: of which I have feene admirable & fuddain effects, even in perfons of 20. or 30. yeares deafeneffe. Make a poffet drinké with one part of a pretty good fpirit of wine & two parts of new milke, throwing away the curde. Before you vfe it, droppe a little oyle of fweete Almends into the deafe eare, & let it foake in, for halfe an hour or an hour, laying that eare in a fit pofture for that effect. Then with a firinge without a little long pipe at the end; but blunt, fo as to fill the orifice of the eare, to keepe the liquour from rebounding too eafily out, inject fome of the poffet drinke luke-warme, do this as often as you fhall fee caufe (not aboue twice at a time; but intermitting halfe a day between) & always when you have done, ftop the eare with blacke wool dipped in a little civet, diftempered with oyle of fweeté Almonds. If both eares needeth cure, apply it to the fecond when the firft hath received its injection. I have feen at the firft fyringing a hard fubftance two Inches long (not vnlike the pith of Elder) ftart out of the eare.

I would be glad to fee an act of Oblivion, or forgetting the moleftation of perfons that have never bin delinquents: *c*. for this is my cafe, as I doubt not of making it appear affoon as it fhall be heard, which is all I Labour for, asking no favour, but only juftice. The act to take away laws againft *Papifts*, concerneth me not, for there never was any proceeding againft me, as a *Papift*, fo that in that regard I ftand *rectus in curia*. Vpon the whole matter I am confident it will not be long before I be allowed to returne home, when one of my greateft contentment will be the happineffe of enjoying

b. I am informed this is a good remedy, & therefore I print it as fuch. For the common good.

c. Here we fee how much he was miftaken, when he boafted fo much of his credit with the prime Rebels: feing

often

he could not obtaîne from them so much as security for his owne person.

d. He continues in his abject sordid flattery.

often your excellent *d.* Conuersation. I wrote to you from hence the 5. of this month, by Mr. *Ayliffe:* & the 7. by *Iohn Lee.* And I have with my tediousnesse trespassed too long vpon you now. And I cannot of a suddaine breake off the conuersation of a person I esteeme, & honor so much, as I do you. I now committ you to Gods blessed Protection, & with all respect do take leave of you & rest

Calis 11. Nou. 1650.   Your most humble & most affectionate seruant

Kenelme Digby.

On the back: To Mr. Jacob Boeve 14. 9ber. 1650.

❖❖❖❖❖❖❖❖❖❖❖❖❖❖❖❖❖❖❖❖❖❖❖❖

Mr. Blacklovv to Sir K. D.

Most honoured Sir   Epist. 46.

Yours of the 12. of Nou. came to me on the 19. the very writing time which made me guilty of my owne slownesse to differr the answer vntill this next post. Your motion of writing a rule of Doctrine is very good & a thing I desire to do before I stire out of *Paris.* But Scheper *Daniel* having brought my packet so late, my hands are at the present full with reading over those papers, which I desire God willing to print in *Paris* by your assistance. Howsoever I desire to make it ready for your syght against you come, that you having perused it we may the better discourse of what is contained in them, whereof you seeme to be curious. In those papers I beleive will bee some things which will make the *Iansenists* in part side with mee, & the treatise you speake of will come out with more authority if the Authour be famed before. Besides this my brother hath written that he thinketh to be shortly heere, & therefore I am not vnwilling to refresh

some

fome geometricall notions, to give him content withall. As for defires of your returne they eafily frame in me without my owne feeking, by the fole power of the obiect. But for hopes of it, I know not how to meafure them, being not able to judge of the circumftances. As for my entertainment, I have more adoe to keepe of exceffe then defect, & nothing is wanting but your company. There lyeth *Rovens* 18. livres for the *Charthufians* of *newport* from Mr. *More* in my command, if I could gett an acquittance for which I have fent often to *Doway*, but get no anfwer. If you can gett their acquittance fent, I fhall fee the monyes delivered heere, or in *Doway*, to whom they pleafe. No more but that I am as ever *Paris* 23. of Nouem 1650.

> Your moft affectionately humble feruant
> Tho.   White

On the back: from Mr. White 23. Nou. 1650.

VVe fee here a defigne to ftrengthen himfelf with the favour of the Ian-fenifts, which thofe Papers would procure him: & he needed not to doubt of the fucceffe, they being ready to joyne with any Novellifts, *to encreafe the Difficultyes againft the Church.*

❖❖❖ ❖❖❖❖❖❖❖❖ ❖❖ ❖❖ ❖❖❖❖❖❖❖ ❖❖ ❖❖ ❖❖❖ ❖❖❖❖❖ ❖❖❖ ❖❖❖

Mr. *Blacklovv* to Sir *Ken. D.*

Moft honored Sir   *Epift.* 47.

Thefe are not to complaine of your long ftay, the which I know to be very neceffary, though vngratefull to him, that feeth himfelf by this meanes to fpend your goods without affording you that comfort you feemed to ayme at in his feruice. But to have your aduice in an occafion propofed

vnto

vnto me from *London.* VVhitaker a ftationer, who printed my
Inftitutiones Peripateticæ is not fo weary of that bargaine,
but that he is willing to print my *Divinity.* Mr. *Auften,* whom
I beleive you remember at *Rome,* promifeth to be the cor-
rectour. I have anfwered for the prefent, I could doe nothing,
becaufe of your abfence, & fome engagement I had put you
into. But being vncertaine of your ftay there, I thought it
good to take your aduice. I am not fond of VVhitaker, for
I faw a copy of my *Inftitutions,* which mee thought were nether good paper, nor correctedly printed. But likewife your
laft letter hath put me out of hart with *leffe,* feing you cha-
racterize him to bee the *proprius* of the *fraterie* which fuppofed
it is impoffible the book fhould not be fuppreffed before
divulged. The reafons for which I defire your prefence before I refolue this affaire are cheifly two. The one to confult what were beft for the book, & the divulging it here:
which I think to bee a circumftance of importance, & may
be beft don now when the *Ianfenifts* begin to print bookes
without approbation. The other is that your felf myght have
the perufing of it whileft I am with you: for befides the
ambiguityes which I myght cleere to you, I apprehend you
may finde in this book what you wrote to me for in *Dovvay:*
for I account tru *Divinity* to be nothing, but the vnueyling
of thofe confiderations which God hath prepared for the fteer-
ing of our foules * to its laft End This is my Propofi-
tion: the Judgment yours, I to obey as
      Your moft affectionate &humble feruant
Decemb. the Laft.   Thomas White.

On the back: from Mr. White 31. Dec. 1650.

* *This is tru, & appeares eminently in the writings of the Fathers, &*
feverall fchoole Divines, if not all. Yet how far Mr. Blacklos Di-
vinity is from that, I refer to the Iudgment of thofe who have reade
it. I never knew any one the better man for reading it. It nourifhes
                                      Pride

Pride, Faction, Contempt of Superiority, ſtubborneſſe in judgment, & will, extinguiſhes feeling Devotion, *& ſenſe of Piety, & diſpoſes to ſchiſme, and hereſy. It may be knowne by its fruits. For amongſt his Diſciples little of tru* chriſtianity *is to be found, whoſe life, is* Charity, *which is baniſh't by a root of* bitterneſſe ſpringing vp out of it, Radix amaritudinis ſurſum germinans. *VVhich is knowne by the perpetuall calumnyes againſt all who diſlike their doctrine, without ſparing even the eminenteſt Men amongſt their owne Brethren, as we have ſeene in Dr.* Holden *againſt Dr.* Leybourne, *& do dayly ſee, & heare in the ordinary diſcourſe againſt* Regulars. *Can the Tree be good, which brings forth ſuch* anti-Chriſtian Fruite ? *See my annotation on Sir K. D.'s Letter 25. Feb.* 1650. *you will there find ſome reaſons, why this man's Diuinity is contrary to tru Piety. Indeed two Paſſions have a maine influence on all our Actions,* Hope *&* Feare *which may be termed the two wheeles, on which all our Affections turne, or the two generall fountaines of all our Actions. By theſe* God *himſelf in his Divine Scriptures Endevours to delarr vs from bad, & ſtirs vs vp to good Actions. (vide Eccli.* 15. 18. *) Setting before our eyes the Greateſt of* Evils, Hell fire *deſgned for the wicked: & the greateſt of good things the* Heavenly Kingdome *prepard for the good, & virtuous. Mat.* 25. 34. *&* 41. *Now this* Hope, *& this* Feare *is extiinguiſht by the Doctrine delivered in this Divinity of Mr.* Blacklo : *which containes nothing, but meere* Philoſophical Notions. *mingled with ſome termes taken out of* Chriſtianity, *or Scripture, but handled more as a proud* Pagan *then an humble* Chriſtian : *& ſavouring more of an Epicurean Libertiniſme, then* Catholick *ſubmiſſion of the vnderſtanding to the yoke of Faith. This ſentiment all muſt frame of it, who read it with a mind not prepoſſeſt ; but at liberty to judge of it, & not all blind ſubmiſſion to his ſentiments, which is due to none but* God, *& his Church.*

❀❀❀❀❀❀❀❀❀❀❀❀❀❀❀❀❀❀❀❀❀❀❀❀❀❀❀❀❀❀❀❀❀❀

Mr. Blacklovv to Sir K. D.

Moſt honored Sir   *Epiſt.* 48.

Theſe are to accompany my Brother for bienſeance, your goodneſſe not permitting that he ſhould need any company. Withall to have aduice about a little treatiſe I intend to print
vnleſſe

a He guesses very ryght: for a spirit of singularity, & Novelty accompanyes him in all his writings: which must needes give occasion of exceptions to Divines; who are taught to tread in the footsteps of their Ancestors, & cundicunt nové, non dicere nova, as Vincentius Lirin.

vnlesse your opinion be contrary. I intend to call it *Institutionum Peripateticarum pars Theorica*, & if you like of it, I would add that it is *admentem* of the authour of the Immortality of the soul. There will be some matter of which our Divines may except against *a.* but peraduenture will not whilest I live out of Action, & therefore I aduertise you, that you be not engaged vnawares, although for all this title you may disavow any part of the doctrin, seing I may mistake your minde. I think the book will be at the hyghest a *Cardescu* book. I could wish therefore to know how many you would advise me to print, 750. or only 100. for frends. This later way the cost will be lesse but wholy lost. The former way, if I can putt them of, there may be some profit. But my writings are such *b.* as take with few. For other things my Brother can give you a better accompt then I whose chief worth is to bee ever, (2. of July)

　　　　Your most humbly affectionate freind & servant
　　　　　　　　　　　　　　　Le Blanc.

Nothing on the back, anciently. I suppose it to be of the year 1651. seing on nou. 23. 1650. he spake of his Brother as to come, who now was past.

Vincentius Lirin. Hath it, to deliver old things in a new manner.

　　b. No great wonder: for he writes vnknowne Doctrines in an vngratefull, insipid stile. Dr. Holden in a letter to Sir K. D. of the 9. of nouem. 1646. says: I feare that Mr. White will neither accept of the place you designe for him, nor will be fit for it. It is lippe learning which prevailes amongst men: & we have so few mortall Angels, that all invisible knowledge is for the Deserts. *Thus he, speaking of the obscure & vnpleasant way of delivering his minde vsed by Mr. Blacklov both in ordinary discourse, & writing. which way rebutes those, who retaine to themselues a Liberty of discerning Gold from Copper, Truth from Fables, yet hath beene of as great vse to entertaine his Disciples in the admiration of his sentiments, when they were but trivial, or worse, as the obscurity of the oracles meeting with minds prepossest with an opinion of their Truth, served to entertain the Deluded Idolaters in that erroneous veneration, altho the answer were such as did not surpasse the reach of an ordinary wit accompanyed with craft.*

❖❖❖❖❖❖❖❖❖❖❖❖❖❖❖❖❖❖❖❖❖❖❖❖❖❖❖❖❖❖❖❖❖

Most noble Sir   *Epist.* 49.

I have received your Letter by my cofen *Dermer*, vpon whom
I have waited every day fince his arrivall at this citty, which
was this day feuernyght, endeavouring to comply with your
commands according to my power. The G. Duke, & his
brother are abfent from *Florence*, & have been fo ever fince
he came, & fo he could not come to kiffe their hands. But
this will be fupplyed at his return, for he intends to paffe
all the fummer in this court. This morning he is gone for
Rome. Thus much touching my cofen *Dormer*, & the obligation I have to ferue him vppon your recomendation. But
there is another favour for which I connot render you fufficient thankes, which is the prefent you were pleafed to
make me of Mr. *Blacklo* his Learned *Divinity* which at laft
I have received together with his other *Opufcula.* I did not
thinke to have given you an account of this, vntill I had
perufed them all; but I find that the worke is too tough,
to be run over curforily, it muft be reade with attention.
I know not how it will relifh amongft our *Italian Divines*,
efpecially when they reade his doctrine of *Purgatorye*: as yet
I hear no talke of it, it feemes either that they have not
feene his book, or els they find it too hard a taske to reade
it over. For my part I do not fee how it can ftand with that
maxime of *Tradition a.* which is the ground of all our beleife:
& although fome of the ancient Fathers myght have beene
of the contrary opinion, *b.* yet that ought not to prejudice
the prefent doctrine which for many ages hath been held
nemine contradicente, & hath beene Confirmed by the v-
niverfall practice of the Church. For vpon the fame ground
it myght be denyed alfo, that the Saints departed fhall fee
God before the day of Judgement, for the fame Fathers
were alfo of that opinion. Secondly *c.* if all fhall remaine in
Purgatory

a. Mr. *Fitton*
diflikes
Blacklo's
opinion of
Purgatory.
His firft rea-
fon.

b. This is
not tru; for
not one of the
Ancient Fa-
thers held
what Black-
low *teaches*
of Puga-
tory.

c. His fecond
reafon.

Purgatory till the day of Judgement, without any alteration for want of their bodyes to worke it, what avayleth it to pray for foules in particular, & yet it hath been practifed in the Church for all ages from the times of the Apoftles. 3ly *d.* Mr. *Blacklo's Purgatory* as I conceive it muft needes be moft grevious to thofe, who have moft *Charity*, & were leffe charged with finnes whileft they lived in this world, in regard that they have a greater defire to fee God, then one who hath leffe charity & confequently a greater pain, then ane, who hath Leffe : & yet the one is to endure as long as the other.

But to let this queftion paffe till I fee Mr. *Blacklos* book, which I vnderftand he hath written of this fubject. I fhall make bold to beg a favour of you for my owne particular, having vnderftood from my cofen *Dormer* that you intéd fhort to fee *England:* wherefore you may be pleafed to know that there is a debt due to me--&c, with my moft humble refpects to your felfe, I remaine Florence 30. oct. 1653.

Your moft humble & moft obliged feruant Peter Fitton.

On the back : from Mr. Fitton 30. 8ber. 1653. Of Purgatory &c.

❀❀❀❀❀❀❀❀❀❀❀❀❀❀❀❀❀❀❀❀❀❀❀❀❀❀❀❀❀❀❀❀

A Letter of the chapter to Abbot Montagu about his being Bishop.

Honourable & Right Reverend.

Epift· 50.

We have according to our Order formerly obferued by our Generall Affemblyes nominated fix to be prefented at Rome
our

out of whom a Bishop is to be elected at his Holinesse his pleasure; & with an vnanimous vote your Honourable Self in the first place. Of whose vnexceptionable worth, & inclinations towards our Chapter, & Body wee have that assured esteeme, that our naming any other besides is rather an effect of our respects to His Holinesse, then a deem'd competition or ballanceing of any second with your worthiest self. We heartily wish there were no more difficultyes to be overcome, then on our sides, where the resolution was so readily, & heartily made, that it was not judg'd worthy to admit any the least debate. Perhaps we may feare some difficulty at Rome to obraine that Authority, which onely we dare admit, that is an Ordinary, or Bishop; but we more fear a modest disinclination on your part; whose very name and Person wee with good reason hope might otherwise bee a meanes to obtaine vs the thing wee sue for. We become therefore humble suppliants to your Lordship by your goodnesse, & by the affection you bear towards vs your Brethrren, (of which we are very confident) that you would please if his Hol. so think good, not to refuse a Charge, for which inward personall Endowments concurring with circumstantiall considerations represents you to the eyes of the world as every way most fit. The rest of our Consultations & Orders, your Lordship will vnderstand from our Common Letter, which accompanys this, & from our Agent, Mr. Holt; whom we have enjoined to communicate our Intentions particularly with your self. Recommending the welfare of our Chapter, & Body to your Lordship's Condescendency to our Petition & your self to the Protection of the Almyghry, we rest

Your Lordship's most affectionate Brethren & most humble servants in Christ

Humphrey Ellis Deane. By order of the Deane & Chapter

Aug. 23. 1667.   John Holland Secretary.

Note: This Letter is a forerunner of severall others, & mentioned in them, & for that reason is here publisht.

❀❀❀❀❀❀❀❀❀❀❀❀❀❀❀❀❀❀❀❀❀❀❀❀❀❀❀❀❀❀

29. July 1667.

My Lord   *Epiſt* 51.

This day only I received your Lordſhip's civill Letter in one from Monſieur *Tilier*, to whom I am extreamely obliged for his civility & curteſyes towards me, in ſo much that I beleive with the helpe of your Lordſhip's intereſt my petition preſented to his moſt Chriſtian Majeſty, & the Queen in order to this Community may find the ſucceſſe we deſire. As to the Information your Lordſhip mentioneth, my Letter to Mr. *Clifford*, & Mr. *Carre* will doubtleſſe afford fullneſſe of ſatisfaction vnto your Lordſhip, & our good frend Dr. *Gough.* As to my proceedings to expulſion, truly tis not in my power to expell *a.* any *Alumnus* without expreſſe order from the Cardinalls of the *Congregation de Propaganda ſide*, to whom I have not hitherto writ, In order to the faction *b.* Mr. *Blacklows* ſpirit (which is crept into this family) has rayſed to expell me, if it had power enough, & really I wiſh it had, for theſe 15. yeares I have beene tormented with it, & would eſteeme my ſelfe happie to be ſeparated, as far, as *Rome* from it : & to that Purpoſe I have for 2. yeares, & more Solicited our Protector, & the fore ſayd Cardinals; but now my deſign is to goe thither my ſelfe, ſince Letters will not prevayle. *Vrget præſentia Turni.* The encloſed *c.* is the paper I offred to be ſubſcribed, & twas rejected. Then I deſired of our ſpirited two ghoſtly *Fathers*, which be the heades of the *Faction*, to refer themſelves to your Lordſhip, Dr. *Gough*, Mr. *Clifford*, & Mr. *Carre.* And'twas replyed ſaying will they refer themſelves to the *Chapter.* Which reply did much diſpleaſe me. Nevertheleſs ſome two days after, they ſignified

vnto

a. That Power was taken from the Preſidents of Doway, Colledge by a decree of the Congregation de Propagandâ, *anno* 1662.

b. Seditious practices of Blackloiſts againſt their Superiours.

vnto me , that they were content to refer themſelves, and write to Mr. *Carre* vnto that effect : but doubtleſs they have not, for they are pinch'd with the paper, & ſeeke evaſion after Evaſion. This day they offred to take the oath of *Pius* 5. *Pope* which importes a *Profeßion of Catholick Faith*. To which I anſwered that I had order from the court of *Rome* to keepe out Mr. *VVhites d.* ſpirit out of the houſe ; but not to offer them *Pius* 5. *Oath*. Yet I wiſh them to write to the Cardinals, & if that would content theire Eminences, it ſhould content me. They be at their wits end, & can invent noe lye, nor plauſible evaſion for their preſervation. And this day they endeavoured to make a quarrell, *e.* ſaying I called them *Schiſmatickes*, for refuſing to ſubſcribe the paper. I anſvered I did not call them *Schiſmaticks*, but that they would be eſteemed for ſuch. And wiſh'd them to conſult the cheife Doctors of our Vniverſity, who I aſſured me would wonder they ſhould refuſe ſuch a paper, & judge it an argument of a *Schiſmaticall ſpirit*. This is all I have to ſay at preſent in order to your Lordſhip's civil letter : relying on your Lordſhip's goodnes, that you will be pleaſed to peruſe what I have ſent to Mr. *Clifford*, & Mr. *Carre*, that is my owne letter, thô diſorderly with my letter directed to the *Chapter*, in anſver to one they writ me, & Mr. *Gage* his Letter writ me from *Rome*, when he was Agent there : & thereby judge how prudently my ſayd Letter to the *Chapter* was made the ground of a *Faction*. I profeſſe *f.* to your Lordſhip ſincerely I had nothing before my eyes , but an earneſt deſire of a good intelligence with the Sea Apoſtolick , & thereby vnion amongſt our ſelves : which will never be , if we continue in this *g. Schiſmaticall exerciſe* of authority & *Iuriſdiction*. I ſay *Schiſmaticall*, which I have always afore concealed : & I thus demoſtrate it to your Lordſhip.

h. Our Biſhop of Calcedon was only *Delegatus habent eam poteſtatem & Iuriſdictionem in Regnis Angliæ, & Scotiæ, quam habent Ordinarij in ſuis civitatibus, & Diæceſibus*. And the Pope as appeares by his *Breve* conferd on him this power of an Ordinary

c. It follows this Letter.

d. Blacklos.

e. They talke of Peace, yet hate it , & baniſh it from all places , where they prevaile ſeeking quarrels, as little agreing with their brethren as with others.

f. Dr. Leybourne's ſincere intentions for the publick good fruſtrated by the Chapter Faction.

g. This is moſt certain.

Ordinary, & consequently this *Ordinary Power* was a *Personall Grace*, which of necessity expired with him. Which our last worthy *Bishop* knew *i.* well: for some yeares before his death, he ordered me, his *Grand Vicar*, as also Mr. *Clifford*, to confer facultyes to the cheife of our *Clergy*, saying: *when I am dead, I know not how they will come by them.* And therefore thought fitting to give them, when he was alive, & in power. Out of these premisses it is Evident, that the *Chapter* did not *succedere in ordinaria Iurisdictione Episcopi defuncti:* that *Ordinary Iurisdiction* in him being a *Personall Grace*, that of necessity expires, the *Bishop* dying. This is the doctrin of all *Catholick, Orthodox Doctors.* But now let vs suppose this ordinary power did not expire in the death of the *Bishop*; & suppose also that his *Chapter* had been Confirmed, & consequently did *succedere in hac potestate Ordinariâ*, neverthelets though it were a Chapter as good & valid, as that of *S. Peters at Rome*, or as that of our *Ladys Church at Paris*, it could not *succedere l. in Episcopi authoritate, & Iurisdictione extraordinariâ*, that is such a *Chapter* could not lawfully exercise their *Bishops Facultyes extra sortem*, granted by the *Pope*, vnless his *Holiness* gave express leave thereunto: & without his sayd *Holiness* Leave, & approbation such exercising of such *Facultyes* is *Schismaticall, erroneous, & Sacrilegious.* But our *Deane & Chapter* exercise our *Bishops* exteroordinary *Facultyes*, give our *Bishops* exteroordinary *Facultyes*, & make *Vicars*, & *Arch-Deacons* as many as they please, without his *Holiness* Leave, having never asked of him either ordinary, or exteroordinary *Facultyes*. When in *England* I demanded of the *Deane*, Dr. *VVarten* allias *Ellis*, *m. quâ auctoritate, quâ Conscientiâ* he could give *exteroordinary*, or indeed *any Facultyes?* he replyed, the *Pope* could not but know what they did: & that was *Sufficient.* My Lord, how deplorable it is, that such a *Clergy*, as we are, should have no better *authority & Iurisdiction*, as to *exteroordinary Facultyes*, then what is *presumtive, & interpretative* onely, *Deus bene in qua tempora seruasti nos!* The thought *n.* of this has given me often a sad heauy heart: & my Lord
I will

I will dy o. rather then breed my Children to ſwear *Obe-dience* to ſuch a *Chapter* : but the two *Conſiſſarij*; which have ſworn obedience p. vnto it, as I am now (too late) certainly informed, have gained the greateſt part of my young *Prieſts*, & *Divines*, to ſide with the *Chapter*. My Lord I have now intrencht on your Lordſhips Patience : & therefore beg your pardon, & ſwear Obedience to your Lordſhips commands, who am in all cordiall manner

> My Lord
>
> Your honours moſt humble & obedient ſervact
>
> Geo. Leybourne.

Hæc raptim.

I would willingly write my Letters twice over, but truly my hand ſhakes, & I am ould.

The writing offered to be ſubſcribed ſent with this Letter. *Infraſcripti Praſes, Profeſſores, & Officiales Pontificij Collegij Duaci declaramus nos eſſe paratos acceptare, & ſpontanèe, & libenter amplexari eam autoritatem, & Iuriſdictionem, quam ſanctiſſimus Dominus Noſter Clemens 9. Papa aſſignavit, & conſtituit pro Regimine Cleri Secularis in Angliâ.*

margin: Divinity, & Canon-Law côcerning the pretended Chapter: who all vnanomuſly (thô vnknown neto one another) anſwered, that the Chapter was Null: which he here hints at. Nay the chief Canons know this nullity, as appeares by the Letter of Mr. Fitton to Sir K. D.

11. Octob. 1647. & the *Petition of the Agent of the* Clergy, *which follows it.*

l. *A third reaſon of illegality of the* Pretended Chapter's *proceedings, their vſurping without any grant from* Rome, *or colour of law, the* extraordinary Facultys *granted by a ſpecial deed to the late* Biſhop. *To which no* Chapter *how Canonical ſoever, ever pretended.*

m. Dr. Humphrey Waren, *alias* Ellis, *acknowledges the nullity of the* Chapter, *of which he was* Dean, *& acted as ſuch, who only pretended the* Pope's *knowledge of what they did. But he did not take notice, that the* Pope *had expreſt frequently, nay on all occaſions, his diſlike of what they did as being* ſchiſmaticall Vſurpation. *VVith a like reaſon the* London Rebels *might have excuſed their ſeditious Actings, becauſe the* King *knew what they did, Indeed that* Rebellion *in the* State *againſt the* King, *& this in the* Church *aginſt the* Pope, *began at the ſame time, (which is worth the noting) & was defended in ſome ſort with the ſame pretences.*

The

-n. The like sadness of hart this consideration would give to all other Clergy-men, *would they weygh the pernicious consequences, which flow from it: viz,* Nullity of Dispensations, Inualidity *of* Absolutions, *&* Sacriledges without number, *of all kinds, which naturally flow from vnlawfull authority, in matters so vnlimited, as they pretend to, & exercise. Let them consider what account they can give to God of the deluded souls, who rely on them.*

o. A zealous resolution in the pious old man.

p. Another sacrilegious practice, to take illegall vows of Obedience *of* Persons, *in opposition to the legall authority of their lawfull superiours.*

Opinion of the Clergy men in Paris Concerning the points in debate in Dovvay Colledge.

1 It appeares vpon reading the papers, & Letters directed to vs from Mr. *President* on the one side, & the *Seniors* of the Colledge on the other side, that both partys have sent their case to Rome: & therefore we judge it altogether improper for vs to pronounce any determinate sentence.

2 It seemes to vs most necessary not only in regard of the vnsetled condition of our *Ecclesiasticall affaires* in *England,* but of the Seasonablenesse of this conjuncture, wherein it hath pleased God to give vs a supreme Pastour, who hath a particular inclination to helpe vs & doth at this present expresse a desire to be informed of our affayres (as we are informed by letters from Rome) that an Agent be sent to his Holines withall possible speed; which Person *a.* cannot appeare vsefully there without carrying with him the signature of some engagement to the effect of this proposed paper, now in question, from the *Clergy of England,* & together with it from the Colledge of *Dovvay,* & that of *Lisbone* also, soon as it may be had.

a. Altho they doe not presume to decide the difference betwixt the two contending partyes, yet they approve what Dr. Leybourne required & tacitly condemne the dissenters.

3. In

3 In purſuance of this opinion of ours, we do preſently write into England, for the haſting away of a fit Agent with ample inſtruction, concerning the ſtate of our affaires & with the afore mentione *Subſcription* of the *Clergy*.

4. In the meane time for the peace of the Colledge, we deſire Mr. Preſident *b.* to ſuſpend the vrging of any ſubſcription, till the Agent be ready to goe with the *Vnanimous ſubſcription* of the *Clergy*, which we hope ſhall be haſtned with all poſſible expedition.

b. **This pro-
viſionall ad-
vice to ſuſ-
pend the ex-
action of the
ſubſcription is
no blame to
Mr. Preſi-
dent who
exacted it;
but only a
ſuſpence of
that affaire,*

Wa. Montagu
    W. Clifford
  Thomas Carre   Stephen Gough.

to auoide greater diſorders, which myght be feared though the refractorineſſe of theſe, who having Vowed illegally obedience to the vſurpation of the Chapter, *did adhere more tenaciouſly to that, then to their Duty their Lawfull Superiours, or the Pope, who appointed them.*

❖❖❖❖❖❖❖❖❖ ❖❖❖❖❖❖❖❖❖❖❖❖❖❖❖❖❖❖❖❖❖❖❖

A Letter from Ab. Montagu to D. Ellis.

Colombe. 27. Sept. 1667.

Mr. Doctor Ellis.   *Epiſt.* **53.**

I have conceived the readyeſt way, to convey my acknow-
legment to all our freinds, *a.* from whom I have received
ſo great a teſtimony of their affection, & eſteeme, is by your
conueyance of my reſentments, relying much vpon your
particular frendſhip for the delivering of them to the beſt
improvement of ſuch a returne, & I muſt entreate you to
repreſent to them the ingenvity of my perſwaſion, which
moves me to decline the Propoſition. I have declared to Mr.
Car at large the reaſons, that move me to this determination,

a. He thanks
the Chap-
ter *for their
kindneß to
him, in nam-
ing him to
his Holi-
neß, for
their future*

5   and

Bishop:
*which he vn-
derstood by
their Letter
of the 23.
August
1667.*

*b. He de-
clines the
Office.*

*c. The intent
of the sub-
scription mis-
understood by
the* Chap-
ter, *as ap-
peared by the
the* Instruc-
tions *given
to Mr.*
Holt.

and as he professes himself satisfyed , so he hath promist me
his offices towards the perswading the rest of our frends of
the justnes of my considerations in the matter : & truly for
no motive but that of securing the cause from prejudices ,
which the notoriousnes of my person , joined with the ob-
noxiousnes of the office doth determine me in the declin-
ing of it.

Wherefore *b.* I am perswaded that vpon full discussion of
the question , you will all conclude my motives to be justi-
fyed by the sight of inconveniences , which are so visible in
the exposure of my person to the view of our aduersarys ,
& as I presume your judgments will conclude with mine ,
in this point , so I must entreate your opinions , to grant
me the beleefe of my gratitude in this occasion & my zealous
application in all occurrencyes , wherein I may hope to
honour & serve there society.

I must now proceede to deliver the common sense of our
brethren here vpon the consulting Mr, *Holts Commißion* and
Instructions : & we conceive you mistake vs much in the end
of our proposall of the signature of that short profession of
obedience to our great superior. The tru intention *c.* on our
part being to conciliate & dispose the power we acknowledge
to determine that sort of Government we all desire , which is
Episcopall , & we are not determined by this civil aduance
of our dutys , to accept that forme , which we intend
to decline as much, as you , so that our propose in this generall submission in our first addresse is to dispose our judge to
conforme his sentence to our conveniences , which is certainly
best provided for by a generall deference to his proposalls ,
which doth not bind vs , as to the first offer , but rather give
vs a justifiable freedome to represent our sense , in what
shall be suggested to vs.

And by this so acceptable entrance into the deliberation
we may be very confident, of a faire proceeding from our
Judge, & of his concurrence with our Unanimous judgement:
& as to the scruple of our being concluded by this civil addresse
in

in what order foever fhall be firft difcourfed, & offered to vs, we anfwer that this dutifull aduance of ours doth but difpofe our fuperior to a faire communication & debate of the matter, & not bind vs vp in the firft ouertures.

For thefe reafons, Sir which leave no apprehenfion of having that government impofed vpon vs, which we doe all vnanimoufly decline, we doe very earneftly propofe *d.* to you againe the fignature of this little fubfcription we fent you: & to prevent all apprehenfion of publick offenfe, in the rendring fuch an act publickly notorious, we have conceived that expedient, which is that the fubmiffion propofed to be figned only by the *Deane* & *Secretary*, as the other addreffes are, & this we vndertake to have approved at *Doway: e.* & we perfwade our felves, that it will be fufficient with our fuperior, & cannot endanger the notoriety you object, as dangerous in this conjuncture.

We therefore pray you to confider whether the propofall be not already in the court we are to pleade, & whither the difficulty of this concurrence will not be ftrayned to a great vndutifullnes, & we pray you to judge what operation this diffenfion in the fubmiffive part will have in a court, to which an intire conformity is appropriated, the debate being thus in argument already vpon the ftage we are to enter, you may eafily conclude what compliance we may hope without this Uniforme refpect & recommendation to our Judge.

We have therefore opend our Judgments freely to *Mr. Holt, f.* who hath vndertaken to reprefent them to you as efficatioufly, as the concurrence of his Judgment with ours can promife, & we aprove fo much your choice in him, as we promife our felves your concurrence with his & our judgments in the matter. Vpon all thefe we are confident of your fending to overtake him with this fubfcription of the *Deane*, & *Secretary*, which may have the fame comprifure of the whole body, as the reft of his credentialls: & we the propofers to you of this facilitation of our common wifhes are fo perfwaded

of

d. He vrges the fubfcriptioni

e. Dr. Leybourne's inclination to Peace on any juft termes, not doubted of.

f. Mr. Holt approved of the reafons for the fubfcription.

of the Piety & Prudence of his proposall, as we will not doubt of your present concurrence wherein if you shall make a diffenting difficulty, we conceive our felves bound to declare to you, that we fhall labour to informe our fuperiors of our *g. Threatens* Judgment, & difavow *g.* our correfpondence with the dif-
not to com- fenting party.
municate And on the other fide, if the paper of fubmiffion be
with the fent to the Agent with the inftruction for demanding a Bi-
Chapter , fhop, we are perfwaded *h.* that by the Queenes mediation
if they perfift with his Holines, & other remonftrances we will offer, that
in their refo- the government you apprehend, will not be fo much as offred
lution not to you, & though we are not ignorant of all the apprehenfions.
fubfcribe. of this conjuncture, yet all circumftances confidered, we are
perfwaded, that your demand of a *Bifhop* ought to be retarded.
h. No danger Thus defiring all poffible difpatch of your anfwer, we reft
to be feared   Your moft affectionate brothers, & fervants
from the
fubfcription. On the back: Copy of the anfwer to the Clergy at London
28. Sep. 1667.   All in Abbot Montagus own hand.

✿✦✿✦ ✿✦

A Letter of Dr. Ellis to Abbot Montagu.

Oct. 3.

Right Honorable.   Epift. 54.

We cannot but much refent, that the concurrence of vnhappy circumftances afford your Lordfhp fo ftrong & en-
a. Of a forcing motives for the refufall of that degree *a.* amongft vs,
Bifhop. the acceptance of which would have rendred vs all moft happy.
Now we muft reft content, that we have difcharged our duty
in offering our Obedience, & in the Satisfaction we receive
of your Lordfhips favorable inclination of making vs partakers

partakers of that happinefs: for which we all returne our moft humble thanks, & gratefull acknowledgments.

We have had divers Confults about that little paper of Subfcription. In the firft confult wee had refolved to comply entirely with your Lordfhips defir, & to figne as you prefcribed, & I my felfe, with the Secretary, had order to figne, & feale it, & fend it away by the next poft. But before the next poft day came, other Chapter men *b.* coming to town, *b. He lays the* it was brought into debate againe, & many difficultyes were *fault on many* moved, fo that we could never come to a refolution of it a- *Chapter-* gaine. Wherefore we bethought our felves of an other, *men which* & concluded in this, which I here fend your Lordfhip: *was but of* which we hope may give fatiffaction. I have not time at pre- *one: whom* fent to give your Lordfhip an account more at large of our *we shall find* procedure: for juft now we ended our confult, wherein it *hereafter to* was refolved: & now my letters are called for. By the next *be mr. Iohn* poft I fhall give your Lordfhip a fuller fatiffaction, & in the *Sergeant.* mean while reft

Your Lordfhips moft obedient fervant

Humphrey Waring

The writing profered by the Chapter.

Ego Onuphrius Ellifus S. T. D & Decanus Capituli Ecclefia c. Thefe two Anglicana, Sede vacante, meo & eiufdem Capituli nomine declaro, nos conditions (videlicet Sacerdotes Catholicos) effe paratos acceptare, & fpontanè make the ac libenter amplexari, in quantum ftatus regni, & res Catholicorum whole fub- permittunt, authoritatem, & Iurifdictionem, quam SS. Dominus nofter fcription in- Clemens Papa nonus affignabit, & conftituet pro regimine eiusdem Ec- fignificant: it clfia Anglicana. being always in their power

to decline any Authority appointed by Rome *on thofe accounts.*

d. They dee not promife to acknowledge any authority to governe the Secular Clergy, or the Chapter, *as refolving to continue in that way of* Independence, *into which they entred on their own heads. Yet the cheif neceffity of a* Bifhop *was that, to prevent all thofe finfull inconveniences, which all good, & zealous men deplore, as well as* Dr. Ley- bourne, *whofe fentiments are expreft in his Letter* 29. Iuly 1667.

❧❧❧❧❧❧❧❧❧❧❧❧❧❧❧❧❧❧❧❧❧❧❧❧❧❧❧❧❧❧❧❧❧❧❧

Ryght Honourable   *Epist.* 55.

By the laſt mondays poſt I gave your Lordſhip a breife account of our reſolves, & encloſed in my Letter a copy of the ſubſcription, we had framed, & ſent to our Agent. I could not then enlarge my ſelfe thrrough want of time : now I ſhall endeavour to give your Lordſhip more ample Satisfaction in the carriage of that buſineſſe.

Immediately vpon the receipt of your Lordſhips Letter, I called a conſult, wherein it was reſolved that we ſhould comply with your Lordſhip's deſire in the ſubſcription : & the Secretary, & my ſelfe had orders to ſigne & ſeale it in the name of the whole *Chapter.* But before the poſt day came other Chapter men coming to towne, it was thought fit, that a buſines of ſo great concerne ſhould be debated in a fuller conſult : & our proceedings authorized with more numerous votes. In this ſecond Conſult ſuch difficultyes were rayſed *a.* against that ſubſcription, that in divers ſuceeding Conſults they could not be allayed : & ſo we were forced to lay it aſide, & frame a nother, which we hoped myght give ſatisfaction. It was vrged that the two laſt generall *Chapters* had voted, & ordred that as far as lay in vs, we ſhould not admit of any extraordinary authority, being Commanded ſo to doe by Superiour Powers. We therefore, as being ſubſtituted to the *Chapter*, had not power to act against their orders : which not withſtanding, we had done, had we ſubſcribed, that we would accept of what his Holynes ſhould in poſe vpon vs. Beſides it was much doubted whether the reſt of our brethren would have approved that ſubſcription, & not have rather hyghly cenſured, & condemned vs for ſuch an attempt : & have ſtood to their former reſolves, & left vs to make good what we had ſubſcribed, which we had obliged our ſelves to

doe

a. By Mr. Sergeant *who would yeild to no reaſon.*

doe. Hence by the rash management of this affayre, we myght have been guilty of a great Schisme, & division b. amongst vs, & whilst we endeavoured to establish our government have quite destroyed it. It was also represented, that if wee made this subscription, it would not Lurke so in darknesse, but that it would come to publick lyght in *Rome*, & thence in *Paris*, *Flanders*, & *England*: & at length the state heere would have notice of it; who having been conscious, that wee had formerly engaged to them, *c.* that wee would not accept of any extraordinary authority, & knowing now that we made this contrary subscription, would looke vppon vs as so many knaves not to be relyed on, & those who hitherto protected vs, would then with good reason desert vs, & leave vs to the fury of our enimes who having even by forgery, & calumnyes *d.* endeavoured to fixe vpon the Catholicks the burning of the Citty, & a hundred treacherous plots, to the end they myght rayse a Persecution against them, would certainly embrace this occasion & make good vse of it, to drive home their designe to their greatest advantage. From hence also would follow, that we should be made odious to all the Catholicks of England, for drawing vppon them so great a mischeife.

This subscription was judged also *e.* of dangerous consequence to our *Chapter*, & *Government*: for we we are not ignorant, that the court of *Rome*, & the Holy *Congregation de Propagandâ Fide* are desirous that all Missionaryes should have a totall, & immediate dependence on them. How then can we be secured, that if wee make that subscription, by which we give vp our own liberty, his Holines will not take vs at our word, & reduce vs to immediate subjection, independent of any other, but himself, by annulling our *Chapter*, or imposing vpon vs a *Vicarius Apostolicus*. Tis tru we doe not so much fear the later, because your Lordship hath engaged your promise to oppose it, & the very constitution of our nation is like to exclude it: but for the former, we have

much

b. Can those le guilty of Division in the state, n ho adhere to the King? Or in the Church, n ho adhere to its head?

e. This is a very remarkable point, discovering a secret never owned by the Party before.

d. VVhat farfetcht reasons are here! And all are non causâ procausâ.

e. Here is the tru, & sole reason of their dissent.

much reason to suspect it will come to passe, when we consider how vnsuitable *f.* this *Chapter* is to the inclinations of the Court of *Rome*, how opposed by Mr. *Leybourne* (who as we are informed was the first author of this *Subscription* out of a designe to ruin it) & other most potent & active adversaries: & how we cannot be confident even of your Lordships Patronage, being you have given vs no promisse to defend the rights of the Chapter; but only to oppose extraordinary authority. That we stand therfore, can be attributed to nothing else, but to Ryght of possession *g.* of which wee cañot be deprived without much disturbance: which if we deliver vp by this subscription, we cannot expect we should receive a refusall of so solemne an offer.

Lastly we considered that the Court of Rome could never in reason *k.* expect such a subscription from us, since it was never heard, or read of, that any Ecclesiasticall body ever offerd vp the like. And indeed it could only suite with those, who after some great schisme, or disobedience to his Holines, were now become very penitent, & sensible of their duty, & by such a subscription would give an outward testimony of it. In vs, who were never guilty of any such crime, it would be esteemed only a fraudulent mask for some designe, especially seing we have so lately made it knowne to his Holines, & the court of Rome by Mr. *Lois* his meanes that our Resolutions were quite opposite to this subscription.

For these motives, my Lord which wee cõceive very rationall, & convinceing, we thought fit to wave that subscription, & so to offer another which myght nether argu vs imprudent nor convince vs to be fraudulent; but yet myght satisfy the just, & rationall expectation of his Holines: the copy of which I have here sent your Lordship. And we hope your Lordship vpon serious reflection will approve of our proceeding. How ever we are confident we shall not be found soe highly criminall, as to deserve that heavy punishment, with which your Lordship is pleased to threaten vs at the end of of your letter, saying that you will informe your superiours of your Iudgment, & disavow all correspondence with the Secular dissenting party. My Lord your judgment, as to the point of Obedience, & Submission to his Holines is the same with ours : for your Lordship is as much resolved to oppose any authority inconsistent with the good of this Kingdome, *l.* as wee can bee. Wee offer only, that your Lordship thinks it most conducing to the end we aime at, to palliate that judgment, with a subscription signifying the quite contrary ; whereas wee apprehending that subscription may involue vs in great mischeife, & prove a snare to entrap vs, thinke best to avoyde it. And with submission to your Lordship's better judgment, I doe not vnderstand how this is a crime, that can deserve so great a punishment as breach of correspendence with vs. Nay I am perswaded, that if his Holines vnderstood, that wee made that subscription, meaning nothing lesse, then what it signifyes (which is the way your Lordship *m.* prescribeth to vs) he would be as much displeased with our Subscribing, as your Lordship now is for the refusall of it.

My Lord, there is not a person in the world, whose good opinion wee should more ambitiously covet, then your Lordships ; whose zeal we have to our great comfort experienced, & whose power we know to be very transcendent. Had not your Lordships demands endangered our very Beeing, wee should not have been backward in complying with them. But when they are of so dangerous consequence, &, as we apprehend, tend to our ruin, let mee humbly beg of your Lordship to give vs the liberty of Vsing our owne reason, & follow the dictamen of it without offence : & obtaine the favour, that this may not be made a crime lessening any of vs in your Lordships esteeme, & in particular

Your Lordships most humble & obedient servant

Oct. 14. 1667.   Humphrey Waring.

My

So that of the Secular Clergy, none, but Mr. Sergeant, acted reasonably.

l. As if that Subscription, which was demanded, was inconsistent with the good of the Kingdome! Or Dr. Leybourne, & the rest, who required it, were not as good Patriots, as the Black-loists who courted the Independants!

m. A biting reproach to Mr. Montagu.

❖❖❖❖❖❖❖❖❖❖❖❖❖❖❖❖❖❖❖❖❖❖❖❖❖❖❖❖❖❖❖❖❖❖❖❖

My Lord *Epiſt* 56.

Your Lordſhips charitable deſignes for the good of our Engliſh Clergy puts me on the confidence of Saluting you, vppon the occaſion of the Subſcription, you will have account of this poſt from Dr. *Ellis.* How much they are obliged to you & I with them as an *Engliſhman,* (though my concerne here be the leaſt *a.*) our humble thanks to you, & our prayers for you, can only teſtify. How many meetings, & what paynes it coſt vs to get a conſent *nemine Contradicente* to the ſubſcription, Dr. *Ellis* may tell your Lordſhip. But becauſe *b.* I ſuppoſe he will not tell you, who vſed all his induſtry to hinder it, I ſhall; that your Lordſhip may have an occaſion to employ a little more of the charity, which put you vppon what you have already done : that the *Clergy* may owe to you not only the having a *Superior,* but alſo their *freedome,* from a *troubleſome c.* ſpirit that diſturbes them.

Their Secretary Mr. *Iohn Holland d.* vſed all the ways poſſible to diſturbe this buſineſſe, for it being reſolved in the firſt Conſult, he & the *Deane* ſhould ſigne it, he when twas ſent to him (for he was abſent) abſolutely refuſed to ſigne it, with a moſt imperious controwling letter, pretending ſtrange *e.* things to the Conſult. Uppon which at a ſecond meeting I declared againſt the proceedings of Mr. *Holland,* & reſolved no more to come amongſt them, *f.* if this buſineſſe paſſed not, nor owne any more of their actions, as long as Mr. *Holland* thus Lorded it over them, for that as I deteſted being a Noveleſt, ſo I abhorred to be ſoe eſteemed : which I ſhould not be able to avoyde, if I continued amongſt them, who ſuffred themſelves *g.* to be lead by Mr. *Holland,* the profeſſed diſciple to Mr. *VVhite.* But Mr. *Ellis* Mr. *Curtis,* & Dr. *Godden* conferring with me the next day, & promiſing all ſhould

a. His greateſt concernes was his Bibloprick in Portugal.

b. This gueſſe was very rational, & tru : for indeed Dr. Ellis never named any one in particular; but charged the diſſent on many.

c. Marke this.

d. Mr. Sergeant.

e. You ſee who is the Authour of all thoſe objections.

bᶜ

be mended, I was prevayled vppon to give them another meeting, where we agreed *nemine contradicente*, vppon the Subscription. The clause *in quantum status regni, & res Catholicorum permittent* was put in by the advice of a great Lawyer, & Eminent Catholick, who was of opinion that without it we myght endanger all. This secret I trusted him with, becaufe he is a person trusteth me with the secrets of his soul, as well as his temporall concernes.

f. Here is another, who refused to communicate with them in busineß as Mr. Montagu, & other Clergymen in Paris had done.

Now my Lord it being thus, that the graveft part, & greateft of the *Clergy* are sensible of the injury they suffer by Mr. *Holland* h. being, especially at this time, *Secretary*, if your Lordfhip with advice of Mr. *Clifford*, & Mr. *Car*, will but cause a letter to be written, signifying how much it is to the prejudice of the *clergy*, that he is in that place, k. Comending Mr. *Leybourne*, as he is, as a fit person for it, I am very well assured it will take effect, & your Lordfhip will have the merit, of setting vs in perfect tranquillity. For that I doe assure your Lordfhip setting him aside, here is a *Clergy* as well stored with able, judicious, vertuous l. persons, & as full of Obedience, & submission to the *Sea Apoftolick*, as I beleive any *Clergy* in the world. I humbly beg your Lordfhips pardon in this & desire you will advice about what is fit to be done with the two persons I named. For my part, who am independent on England I am vnconcerned: but ftill as an Englifh man, & Brother feing things tending fo profperoufly to quiet, & eftablifhment, & that only this thing is wanting to perfect it, I confeffe I could not containe my pen (though I incur the cenfure of a too forward perfon) from letting fall fró it to your Lordfhip thefe Lines, the trouble whereof your owne charitable goodneffe has drawne on you. Thus comending this bufineffe to your Charitable onfideration, & your Perfon to the fountain of Charity, I reft

g. The chapter governed, & controuled by Mr. Sergeant, the profeft difciple of Mr. White.

h Moft of the Clergy difpleafed with Mr. Holland's being Secretary to the Chapter.

My very good Lord
Your Lordfhips moft devoted & Humble fervant
Rich. Ruffell.

This

k. **Mr. Ser-** *This Letter hath no date, but by its contents it appeares to have been*
geant *was* *written on the same day, with the latter of Dr. Ellis Dean of the*
shortly after *Chapter, that is,* Oct. 14. 1667.
displaced, &

Mr. John Leybourne *put into his office, probably upon the Letter, which was demanded.*

Here *we see the tru cause of* Sergeant's *being deposed, which was not by his own request, that he myght attend to his controversy writings, contrary to the vnanimous desire of the* Chapter *which was very well satisfyed with his carriage in it, as was alleadged, as I heare, in the* Attestation *produced against the* Arch-Bishop *of* Dub-hill *signed by Dr.* Waring, & Dr Godden; *but because many of the prime* Chapter men *could no longer brooke his insolent controuling humour, nor endure his erroneous sentiments. I am sorry, that those able men* Dr. Ellis, & Dr. Godden, *should give such ground To surmise, they have little regard to Truth, in the Attestations they giue.*

l. That there are very many such in the Secular Clergy, *who deserve this character. I gladly beleive: I wish the management, & direction of its affayres were put into the hands of such, & others, of contrary Principles were not employed in all places of Trust, or at least that they were so far discountenanced, as to prevent that generally malignant Influence they have on all transactions of common concerne. For whilest these are permitted their full swing, their stubborne resolutions, & violent carriage doth disharten moderate, & Orthodox non firm defending the better Part, & forcibly draw them either to a reall or seeming consent, to what they inwardly dislike: As Bishop* Russel *complaines that Mr.* Sergeant (*he alone, & against all the* Chapter-men, *assembled) did by huffing, & bullying in the businesse of the* Subscription. *So Factious men make a figure, & honest men are meere cyphers, whose value depends on the figure, & standes them selves for just nothing.*

F I N I S.

Faults in the Printing.

PReface lineâ 2. *ſecular men. r. ſecular clergy men.* Page 19. l. 17. *your houſe, r. that houſe.* Page 35. *fine: the ſame. r. the ſame, viz. to get all Regulars baniſht.*

P. 40. *linea* 30. *heretical authority, r. ſpiritual authority.*

P. 41. L. 23 *to ſtay. r. to eſſay.*

P. 46. L. 2. *knoweth with. r. knoweth well.*

P. 47. L. 17. *feare r. teare.*

P. 49. L. 10. *carry fauour. r. curry fauour.* Ibidem L. 3. *of the King. r. to the King.*

P. 57 L. penult. *Although &c. r. Although I ſuppoſe the greateſt oppoſition proceedes from Regulars, out of animoſity. The things that exception is taken againſt, are, 1.*

P. 65. L. 2. 17. r. 17. *Ian.*

P. 97. L. 14. *forward. r. froward.*

P. 98 L. 11. *children. Add: Have you ſeen Gregorius à S. Vincentio de Quadraturâ Circuli.*